Wisconsin CURIOSITIES

Quirky characters,
roadside oddities &
other offbeat stuff

3rd Edition

Michael Feldman and Diana Cook

Guilford, Connecticut

The prices, rates, and hours listed in this guidebook were confirmed at press time. We recommend, however, that you call establishments to obtain current information before traveling.

To buy books in quantity for corporate use
or incentives, call **(800) 962-0973**
or e-mail **premiums@GlobePequot.com.**

"Poniatowski" words and music by Peter Berryman © 1988 L & P Berryman

Photos by Diana Cook unless otherwise noted

Text design: Bret Kerr
Layout: Casey Shain
Project Manager: John Burbidge
Maps: Daniel Lloyd © Morris Book Publishing, LLC

Library of Congress Cataloging-in-Publication data is available on file.

ISBN 978-0-7627-4818-1

Printed in the United States of America

10 9 8 7 6 5 4 3 2 1

★ ★

"Curiouser and curiouser!" cried Alice.

—Lewis Carroll, *Alice in Wonderland*

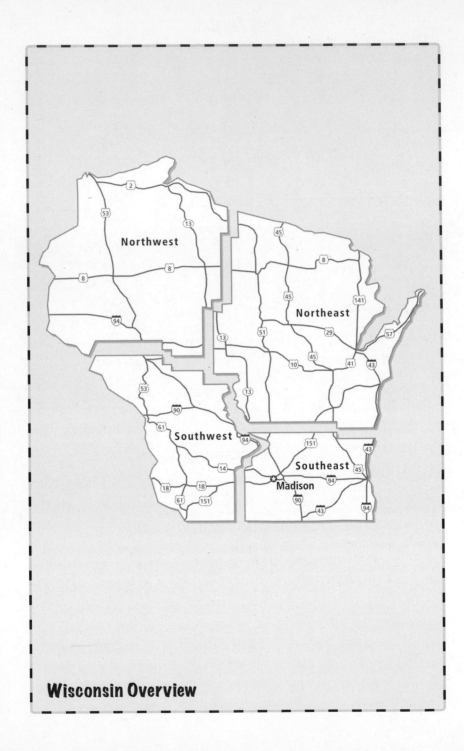

Wisconsin Overview

contents

acknowledgments

★ ★

It was a pleasure to encounter many helpful people throughout Wisconsin in the course of this search for the unique, the unlikely, the delightfully strange, and the positively odd. These fine people include:

People with cameras who know how to use them. Erica Schlueter was a fine photographer, an artist with a keen eye for surprises along the road, and a navigator with solid map-reading skills. Andy Kraushaar anticipated this project by long ago photographing just what the book needed. He then generously shared his work. Jim Legault was the same way.

People who know the territory or know someone who does. For instance, although Barb at the Iron River tourism office hadn't heard about the giant twine ball, she thought Bev at the historical museum 2 blocks over might know. Bev was not familiar with the twine ball, but she knew who would be: Joe at the retirement center in Lake Nebagamon. And sure enough, Joe knew exactly where it was, and he didn't mind taking the time to locate the spot on the road map, even at the risk of missing a historic baseball moment on TV . . . These are our people.

Thanks also to the Wisconsin Department of Tourism for providing photographs. If you'd like assistance in planning your travels around our fair state, call (800) 432-TRIP or check out the Web site at www.travelwisconsin.com.

We love to fish. ANDY KRAUSHAAR

introduction

★ ★

Wisconsin is pretty much the way things should be.

If you want woods, you go up north; for the Great Lakes, head east. The majestic Mississippi River configures our western boundary. And if for any reason you want to go to Illinois, simply point yourself south, but make sure to bring lots of change for the tolls, and remember that you can quickly return to our free and well-maintained highways for safaris to the interior of the Badger State.

Already blessed simply by being a native of Wisconsin (and don't kid yourself, it gives you a leg up on the wheeler-dealers from either coast), I was doubly lucky in having a father, David A., who believed that vacations should be educational. Broadly interpreted, that meant that visiting the world's largest fiberglass muskellunge (in Hayward) could be considered a learning experience.

Dad thought that it was important for kids to step on board the submarine in Manitowoc, to stumble across Al Capone's hideaway in the Northwoods, and to realize what one man carrying bricks on his back up a mountain (only slightly more ambitious than some of Dad's home projects) could build—namely, the cantilevered House on the Rock, made specifically to house the world's largest calliope collection (now a destination of its own in Spring Green). The Wisconsin Dells was our Amazon, the Chippewa Flowage our bayou, the Apostle Islands our Caribbean. Door County was our Cape Cod (even better, since there is no Packer Hall of Fame anywhere near Nantucket), Little Norway our Big Norway, and it's a fact that there are more miles of sand-duned beaches between Marinette and Kenosha than on the entire Côte d'Azur. And as Dad liked to say, it's a lot more convenient.

We would make forays all around the state. Dad was perhaps the first CPA to visit many of the villages where whitefish cheeks were a delicacy, as well as the endless number of fishing lakes where bass (the largemouth variety, not Abe Bass, our dear uncle in scrap metal) leaped into the boat, attracted by the cigar smoke. (Dad never actually did fish; he just sat in the boat smoking his cigar, safe in the knowledge that Mother was hundreds of miles away from smelling it.)

We hunkered down into cabins shaped like cement tepees, along main streets that still looked like Swedish frontier towns except for (or perhaps because of) the chainsaw-carved trolls lining the streets (Mount Horeb). We wandered onto reservations and through national forests. We were transported back in time to Belgian, Norwegian, German, Finnish, Cornish, and French towns founded by people trying to cover up the fact that they had emigrated. We ate our way through the diverse ethnic neighborhoods of Milwaukee, Racine, and Kenosha, and along the many stops of the Frank Lloyd Wright trail of beautiful land-hugging designs and leaky roofs.

Billboard on Highway 35 south of Hudson. ERICA SCHLUETER

introduction

★ ★

If Dad is the inspiration, Diana Cook is the real heroine of this volume, having crisscrossed Wisconsin's class B highways in search of elusive cat-whisker collections and cows with portholes in their stomachs (just one of the many options you can get with your cow in Wisconsin). Her travels have not been without reward. Along the way she teamed with a rural mail carrier to win the mixed doubles Seed-Spitting Championship at the Pardeeville Watermelon Festival, and for her efforts she now has a trophy—presented by Alice in Dairyland—resembling the Stanley Cup. She deserves that and more for her delightful investigative work deep into the heart of Dairyland.

I myself participated in the Prairie du Sac Cow Chip Throw one year, but I didn't even place. The old-timers say the trick is finding the cow chip with just the right moisture content, but I think some of the guys just know which Holstein to back.

We hope you'll find this guide to Wisconsin curiosities both fun and, as my father would maintain, educational, and that it will inspire you to pack up the Taurus wagon and explore our beautiful state. And if you find something a little bit out of the ordinary that we didn't, let us know—Wisconsin surely has many more secrets yet to reveal.

Michael Feldman

Her real name is Wisconsin, but everybody likes to call her Ms. Forward, because she represents the state motto, "Forward." She has a "W" on her chest, an ear of corn behind each ear, and a badger on her head. She left the ground in July 1914 and has been perched atop the capitol dome in Madison ever since. The badger's rear end is the highest point in Madison. WISCONSIN HISTORICAL SOCIETY

How to Tell
Wisconsin
from Minnesota

None of the curiosities described in this book will do you any good if you
go looking for them in Minnesota, but due to what seems to be universal
confusion or a muddying of our border waters, many of you may well
do that. Don't. It would be a mistake. Minnesota already gets all the
attention, what with former governor Jesse Ventura and Garrison "the
shy guy" Keillor. But Wisconsin is really where it's at, which is, facing the
map with your nose pressed to the Mississippi River, on the right. True,
Minnesotans and Wisconsinites are pretty similar. They're probably even
close enough genetically to mate, although you'd be taking a chance.
Maybe they're too close to mate. Minnesota claims 10,000 lakes, but
Wisconsin has at least that many that we don't even talk about because,
in Wisconsin, we think things speak for themselves, so we don't have to.

Wisconsinites and Minnesotans share a common heritage, having
been overrun by the French, who loved us only for our furs, then by
Scandinavians looking for a fjord to ford and Germans who couldn't
cross a creek without wondering what kind of beer it would make.
Neither of us are strangers to biting flies, Lutheran circles, garage art,
covered dishes, Native American casinos, bingo in the church basement,
lawn edging, and what outsiders might take for an unseemly interest in
bovine growth and reproduction. We both keep herring in the house,
and we both know that lefse is to be held like a cigar and that lutefisk
and head cheese are not for the faint of heart. Yahtzee, euchre, and
sheepshead will get you through a long winter night in either place as

1

★ ★

Lucinda wannabes. A Marathon County Holstein named Lucinda holds the world record for milk production. In 1997 she produced 67,914 pounds of milk, which averages out to twenty-two gallons of milk a day, four times more than the average cow. She was owned by Floyd and Lloyd Baumann and Fred Lang of Marathon. WISCONSIN DEPARTMENT OF TOURISM

long as there's a brewski and a bowl of cheese curds for sustenance. Sturdy European stock furnished us both, though we in Wisconsin have been stereotyped as being the larger, when, in fact, we are simply big boned, with the accompanying nice personalities. They say in Minnesota that when offered something, you refuse three times before accepting; in Wisconsin, I've seen it run up to six or seven offers, depending upon what it is.

To the contiguous forty-six states, Minnesota and Wisconsin overlap: People are always calling Kirby Puckett the unofficial mayor of Milwaukee, or tagging Fred MacMurray as the pride of St. Olaf's, much to the chagrin of the alumni of Carroll College in Waukesha, Wisconsin. Historically, the confusion stems from the great tree steal of 1846, when the lumber barons pulled Wisconsin's rug out from under the plat where Minneapolis and St. Paul now stand and lopped off the upper peninsula (currently of Michigan) like a giant appendix. Had they not been wrested from us, the Twin Cities would still be Pig's Eye and St. Anthony's Falls and suburbs of Hudson, Wisconsin, where Cray Super Computers got their start despite Minnesota's claim to be "The Brainpower State" (with billboards on the border facing us!).

Why then, given the commonalities, the shared history and heritage, and the fact that nobody can tell us apart, do we in God's Country (technically just La Crosse, but why confine Him?) continue to feel like Roger Clinton or a pillow stuffed with unknown fiber? Are we the former East Germany to Minnesota's former West? Why do we feel inferior even though some of us are living in Superior? Are the citizens of Minnesota's Lake Wobegon more perfect?

Perhaps it's just a difference in style. For example, the dual burghers of Kenosha/Racine, Neenah/Menasha, and Sauk City/Prairie du Sac, Wisconsin, would never dream of referring to themselves as the "Twin Cities," as residents of Minneapolis/St. Paul do. We know for a fact that there are others, including the Quad Cities (which, with two pair, win). Maybe it's the Cheesehead thing, which only recently occurred to us to be an insult, depending on who says it. Maybe it's just the way Minnesotans stand out like sore thumbs when they cross over in their painfully coordinated colors with names like periwinkle and sage, and in parkas that look like they've never been worn before, let alone to change the oil. Fording the St. Croix is not exactly crossing the Uatuma in Brazil, but in the interests of peace in the neighborhood and upholding the sovereignty of the great state of Wisconsin, here are ten ways to tell that you're in Wisconsin and not Minnesota:

1. People are driving 55 mph in the passing lane. It's well within our rights; after all, the minimum is 40, so we're actually speeding. They raised it to 65 in spots, but that's not our problem. Unlike those fleeing Minnesota to their cabins in Wisconsin, we're in no hurry to get anywhere. Plus, hit a deer at 55 and chances are good that one or both of you will walk away.

★ ★

The Infinity Room at House on the Rock. WISCONSIN DEPARTMENT OF TOURISM

2. Speaking of cabins, you know that you're in Wisconsin if you see an SUV with Brainerd (Minnesota) plates backing up a bass boat to the lake. What with only 10,000 lakes (many scarcely more than puddles) and an average of 100 cabin sites per, there are only 1 million indigenous cabins for 4 million Minnesotans—a shortfall of some 30,000 lakes that they're not going to find in landlocked Iowa.

3. We don't brag about our children's SAT scores in Wisconsin, and not because they don't have them. While Minnesotans may edge us out in some tests, you tell me who the Minnesota Multiphasic Personality Inventory is geared toward.

4. If it's "come as you are," it's Wisconsin. The knockoff Italian double-breasteds and off-the-shoulder cocktail dresses favored in some places don't cut it here. While the state motto is "Forward," it may

as well be "Whatever's Clean." When we say "dress," we mean "wear clothes."

5. If people don't go outdoors in winter, you're in the Twin Cities, scurrying through the skyways like gerbils in a maze. Cold doesn't faze us here—that's why we even bother to ask, "Cold enough for you?" It's not meant to be ironic. If we don't get out in the cold, our winter coats dull and we start to shed. If you need skyways, Madison has as fine a web of steam tunnels as you could hope for, and Milwaukee is the Venice of alleys. Up north you can always find a snowmobile trail and flag somebody down.

6. If you're halfway between the equator and the North Pole and a quarter of the way around the world from Greenwich, England, you're in the capital of the northwestern world: Poniatowski, Wisconsin. This is just one example of how unexpected Wisconsin can be—from the world's largest ginseng fields in Marathon County to the rumored site of the Garden of Eden in Galesville (from which, when Adam and Eve were expelled from Paradise, they emigrated to Minnesota). This book is filled with things that you are simply not going to find in Minnesota: the world's largest talking cow, in Neillsville; the largest loon, in Mercer; the largest six-pack, in La Crosse; the largest M, in Platteville (which at 400 tons would crush any letter in the Hollywood Hills); and the four-and-a-half-story muskie, in Hayward, from whose jaws, if your wife gets down low enough to take the picture, you can appear to be dangling. Two can play at this "world-class" game.

7. If you show up with your spouse and no one else at a restaurant or coffee shop and the girl asks you "How many?" you're in Wisconsin. We take nothing for granted. If you insist on waiting for a booth, don't block the cigarette machine. Don't ask to see the menu before you sit down—it's not going to change things any, and the waitstaff resents it. If you're here on business, please remember that we don't "take a lunch" in Wisconsin, we eat one, and we'll be happy to chat after the fried ice cream.

★ ★

Larry Primeau of De Pere mounted a deer rack to a 1960s Packer helmet and became the Green Bay Packalope. Green and gold Mardi Gras beads (recalling the Super Bowl XXXI victory in New Orleans) and a mini-cheese wedge complete his ensemble. He represents the Packers in the Hall of Fans wing of the Pro Football Hall of Fame in Canton, Ohio. ANDY KRAUSHAAR

8. "Uff da!" and similar Norwegian exclamations occur in both states, but clearly Wisconsin is where a water fountain is a "bubbler" and "Ain'a hey" is the equivalent of "Mon Dieu!" If possible, begin all stories with "So I says . . .," and make sure it's one worth telling: We have very high standards.

9. Wisconsin, the Côte d'Azur of the upper Midwest, averages 2 to 4 degrees Fahrenheit warmer than Minnesota, and 360 degrees warmer than the dark side of Mercury (not counting wind chill), so pack accordingly.

10. You may be able to find a pair of fish cheeks in the land of the Golden Gopher, but fish boils come from Door County, Wisconsin,

a fact that so many Minnesotans and others are aware of, it's getting impossible to get into one. So you might just want to head out to the deck with a large kettle, half a face cord of oak, a dozen small red potatoes, one and a half pounds of small onions, a cheesecloth, eight quarts of water, a pound of salt, two or three pounds of fish steaks, one cup of butter, a pile of lemon wedges, and a couple quarts of kerosene, and take things into your own hands. Since this is a potentially fatal combination, however, feel free to call and we'll talk you down—or, better yet, come by the house and we'll head for the White Gull.

Sixteen-foot, one-ton Claire d' Loon emphasizes Mercer's boast as the Loon Capital. WISCONSIN DEPARTMENT OF TOURISM

1

Northwest

The northwest section of Wisconsin is extremely watery. Not only is it bounded on the north by Lake Superior and on the west by the St. Croix and Mississippi Rivers (except for a 40-mile stretch where Minnesotans and Wisconsinites could, if they chose, stand cheek to jowl), but it has zillions of lakes and rivers. During summer you will notice that many people have fishing poles on their shoulders or canoes on their heads. In winter, when all the water is frozen, they continue fishing by drilling holes in the ice.

This part of Wisconsin is also very woodsy. The Chequamegon-Nicolet National Forest alone covers a million and a half acres (and includes 600 of those lakes). On a Saturday in February, thousands of cross-country skiers from all over the world race through the woods from Hayward to Cable in the 51K Birkebeiner, the largest cross-country ski marathon in North America. They recall the birkebeiner skiers who, in the year 1206, skied through the rugged forests of Norway to smuggle the illegitimate son of King Sverresson and Inga of Vartieg to safety. Today's skiers wear spandex instead of birkebeiners (birchbark leggings), but they have the same desperate and determined look in their eyes.

The most populous place in the northwest section of Wisconsin is the city of Eau Claire, with 61,000 people. But for the most part, there is more space where no one is than where someone is, and that is what makes the northwest what it is.

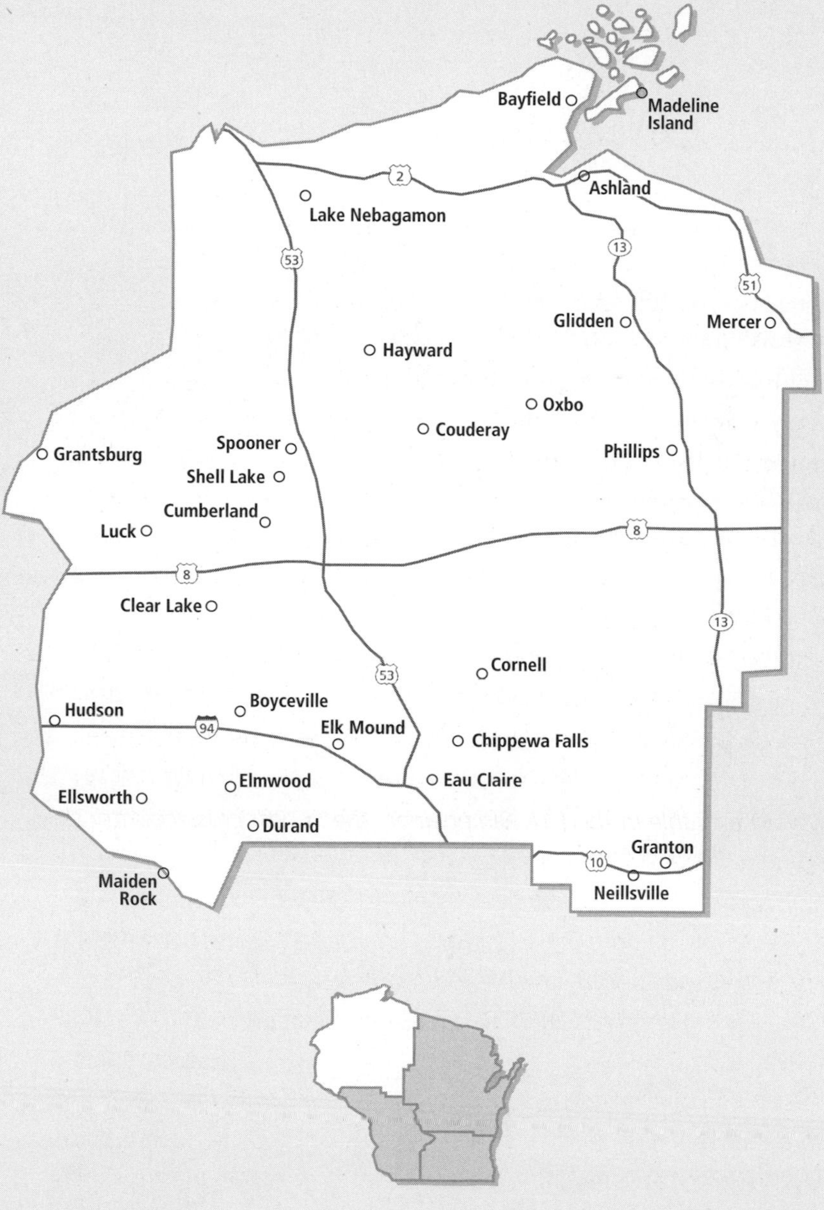

Bayfield
Madeline Island
Ashland
Lake Nebagamon
2
53
13
51
Glidden
Mercer
Hayward
Oxbo
Couderay
Spooner
Grantsburg
Shell Lake
Phillips
Cumberland
Luck
8
Clear Lake
13
Cornell
53
Hudson
Boyceville
94
Elk Mound
Chippewa Falls
Elmwood
Eau Claire
Ellsworth
Durand
Granton
10
Maiden Rock
Neillsville

Northwest

★ ★

The Difference Is, Gaylord Nelson
Couldn't Throw a Spitter to Save His Life
Clear Lake

The Clear Lake Museum proudly—and somewhat incongruously—
presents Burleigh Grimes and Gaylord Nelson, two sons of Clear Lake
who became famous. But neither one of them ever got too big for the
town.

Grimes grew up on a farm nearby, walked to school across Clear
Lake during the winter, played on the Clear Lake Red Jackets, and
ended up in the Baseball Hall of Fame as one of the great spitball
pitchers. In fact, he was the last pitcher to throw legal spitballs (balls
that have been spat upon or somehow moistened to make them break
more sharply). Baseball outlawed them in 1920 but exempted the seventeen pitchers in the major leagues who depended on them for their
livelihood, such as Grimes. "Ol' Stubblebeard" (he didn't shave on days
he pitched) outlasted them all, frightening hitters until 1934, when he
retired. "[Grimes] walked with a swagger that infuriated batters, and
when he measured a hitter from the mound he would peel back his
lips to show yellow teeth in a snarl," wrote the *New York Times* in his
obituary in 1985.

Among a great deal of memorabilia are his St. Louis Cardinals
and New York Yankees uniforms, a baseball autographed by Herbert
Hoover, and his personal license plate, BAG 270 (Burleigh Arland
Grimes, 270 winning games).

A sportswriter once said, "Let's see, Mr. Grimes, you were from a
small town up in northern Wisconsin, Clear Lake?" Replied Grimes, "If
you were good enough, you were from Clear Lake."

Gaylord Nelson was good enough to become governor of Wisconsin
(1959–63) and U.S. senator (1963–81), and to earn a spotless reputation in both public and private life. The son of a local doctor, he grew
up exploring the wilderness at the end of Clear Lake's Main Street. He
took his love of Wisconsin's great outdoors to Washington, sponsored
environmental legislation, and founded Earth Day. President Clinton

Wood from When the Earth Was Young

Diving in the chilly depths of Chequamegon Bay, in Lake Superior off Ashland, is a bit like peering through a telescope pointed at the far end of the galaxy: You can see things that no longer exist. In this neck of the woods, that means submerged logs from the primeval forests of Wisconsin—slow-growth oak, cherry, maple, birch, elm, bird's-eye maple—perfectly preserved by the frigid, low-oxygen waters. These tens or perhaps hundreds of thousands of logs are what remain of virgin forests cut and floated to mills long gone; in the 1870s and 1880s, these were the stands felled to rebuild burned-out Chicago.

This was timber already old when it was cut more than a hundred years ago—350-year-old maple, for example, of a quality no longer seen anywhere, except perhaps in a Stradivarius. (In fact, some of the interest in the maple "sinkers" comes from instrument makers hoping to duplicate violins with wood very much like that which the master used; if Stradivari himself is preserved down there, they may have some luck.)

Timeless Timber, a company in Ashland that hoped to retrieve 20,000 to 30,000 logs a year from the bay, suffered a setback when the Red Cliff band of the Lake Superior Chippewa objected to their removal under nineteenth-century treaties. All future reclamation will be done with the cooperation of the tribe and the U.S. Army Corps of Engineers. But after all, the forest primeval has waited this long—it can wait a little bit longer. You can read more about this once-lost treasure at www.timelesstimber.com.

★ ★

thanked him with the Presidential Medal of Freedom, and in 1999 the National Audubon Society named him and Theodore Roosevelt the two most influential environmentalists of the twentieth century. The museum focuses on his career and includes some childhood items.

The Clear Lake Museum is in an old brick schoolhouse at 450 Fifth Avenue. The curator is Charles Clark, who knew Grimes and Nelson well and says of them both, "You couldn't meet a nicer guy." For information and hours call Mr. Clark at (715) 263-2042.

Thanks So Much, Ezra
Cornell

The city of Cornell is quietly proud to be the home of the last pulp-wood stacker of its kind in existence. It holds no annual Stacker Fest, crowns no beauty queen Miss Stacker, sells no stacker key chains or oven mitts. The Stacker Café on Bridge Street honors it with a break-fast combo called the Main Stacker and labels its restrooms Stacker Jacks and Stacker Jills, but otherwise this enormous monument to the area's logging era has retired with dignity.

For almost sixty years, until 1971, the 175-foot stacker rumbled and clanked year-round. Logs arrived by river and rail, and the stacker was the mechanical middleman that sent them on their way to the paper mill. Down below, it was a labor-intensive operation and a chancy one, with guys feeding all those millions of logs to the stacker and later steering them through the sluiceway.

It's interesting that the small town of Cornell in Wisconsin and Cornell University, the Ivy League school in Ithaca, New York, are named for the same guy. In 1865 Ezra Cornell came to town, then called Brunet Falls, in search of an investment to finance the new university he'd started out east. The pine forests seemed like a promising investment, and he ended up practically owning the Chippewa Valley. He bought 100,000 acres at 50 cents an acre, which before long he parlayed into $6 million for Cornell University's endowment fund. Even though Cornell never hung around long enough to set up residence here, and

Now silent, the stacker made a lot of racket in its day.

★ ★

even though pioneer Jean Brunet did all the hard work up front to earn the title "Father of the Chippewa Valley," Brunet Falls changed its name to Cornell. Funny how things work out that way.

The stacker stands in Cornell Mill Yard Park, at the intersection of Highway 178 and the Chippewa River. The visitor center and Native American museum in the park has historical displays and information. Open mid-May to mid-September from 10:00 a.m. to 4:00 p.m. Monday through Saturday, noon to 4:00 p.m. Sunday. For more information call (715) 239-3619 or (715) 239-3710 or go to www.cityof cornell.com/tosee/centervoice.htm.

When the Bears Paid for Protection
Couderay

Al Capone was nothing if not diversified: bootlegging, gambling, vice, racketeering, bumping off guys, fishing. If he had only paid his taxes, he might be here today, in his 500-acre retreat in the cool and stately pine-and-hardwood forest near Couderay. The wily traveler can find it by following the neon sign that says AL CAPONE'S HIDEOUT. In his day, however, this Northwoods pied-à-terre was so low-profile that even Mrs. Capone didn't know about it. Of course, she may have been the last to know.

To make sure that no one disturbed his peace and quiet and fishing, Capone built a gun tower—unusual in the Northwoods at the time— as well as outbuildings with walls 18 inches thick, and a jail cell for unwelcome visitors. Little did the local tradesmen and craftsmen who hauled all that fieldstone in the 1920s know who they were working for, or so they said.

In 1931 "Public Enemy Number One" had to hang up his fishing pole and head for prison for income-tax evasion—not as colorful a rap as some others that the feds might have pinned on him, but sufficient to keep him off the streets for the next eight years.

Guided tours include the grounds and the main lodge, with its spiral staircases, deer-horn fixtures, and slightly salacious mannequins

★ ★

Trivia

The village of Luck was once the yo-yo capital of the world. In the 1950s and '60s, the Duncan plant in Luck used the area's hard maple trees to produce millions of yo-yos.

perched on the beds. The garage (with four built-in gun portholes) that used to house long black limousines is now a restaurant and bar.

Really well hidden. From Hayward take Highway B to NN to N to CC . . . et cetera (17 miles). Or, from Highway 70 at Couderay, go north on Highway CC (6 miles). Tours from noon to 6:00 p.m. daily, Memorial Day through Labor Day; 11:00 a.m. to 5:00 p.m. for three-day weekends through October. Admission is charged. For more information call (715) 945-2746 or visit www.alcaponehideout.com.

The Rutabaga-Free Festival
Cumberland

They've taken the rutabaga out of the Rutabaga Festival. The bland and homely root vegetable—something like a cross between a cabbage and a turnip—is no longer the big cash crop that it was in these parts when the festival started, back in 1932. Gone are the days of the rutabaga bakeoff and the rutabaga cookbook. And if they talk about them at all, they call them "baggies." Even the festival queen is crowned "Miss Cumberland," not "Miss Rutabaga."

You can take the rutabaga out of the festival, but you can't take the festival out of Cumberland. The festivities carry on for four days over the weekend before Labor Day, with a parade, live music, a hot-pepper-eating contest, a pancake breakfast, and an ice-cream social. But, except for an occasional bold entry—like rutabaga cheesecake or

★ ★

This 1940s red Farmall H tractor is no ordinary tractor-on-a-post. It rotates, and at night its lights sweep across the sky. The handy landmark is at 8892 Highway 178 near Chippewa Falls. Its creator, Bill Goulet, says it also makes a good birdhouse. COURTESY BILL GOULET

rutabaga bratwurst—barely a nod to the humble rutabaga.

For details about the Rutabaga Festival, call (715) 822-3378 or visit www.cumberland-wisconsin.com.

The town of Boyceville also celebrates a phantom vegetable. Although the pickle factory left a few years ago, the Cucumber Festival goes on, at least in name. A grand parade and a treasure hunt for the Golden Pickle are just two events of the three-day festival in August. For more information see www.boycevillewi.com.

★ ★

Run Bambi, Run!

Durand

Anna Mae Bauer has had eighteen collisions with deer on the road. "It's not as if I'm out to set a record or anything," says Anna Mae, who probably has set a record.

Nevertheless, the intrepid Anna Mae continues to drive nearly 500 miles a week between her home in Durand and her job in Chippewa Falls. Traveling a heavily wooded highway somewhat increases the odds here.

Not all the deer were killed on the spot. Number One (sometime in 1958) was just dazed a little; others have been able to stumble away into the woods.

As a regular customer, Anna Mae now consults the guys at G&W Body Shop in Durand before buying a new car, anticipating the need to match paint and so on. And she has high praise for her insurance company, though on occasion she's been too embarrassed to file yet another claim.

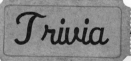

Trivia

The bumper stickers read REAL TOURISTS EAT WHITEFISH LIVERS because Bayfield discovered that if you stop calling them fish guts, you can sell them to tourists as a real delicacy. Restaurants sauté them in butter, sometimes combined with red peppers and onions or with bacon, onion, and mushrooms. The Norwegian way is to stew them in milk. ("They like to have all their food white," explains one chef.) Gourmet shops sell them pureed in a pâté. Local fish markets sell them straight, for those who want to rustle up a batch at home.

★ ★

For a while she had four or five deer alerts attached to the front of her car. They were supposed to warn deer of her approach, but the animals leaped into her path anyway—and took the devices with them as they went down. Anna Mae does not invest in deer alerts anymore.

Deer Number Seventeen had a curious response. As Anna Mae got out of the car and approached, the deer raised its head and gazed at her, as if to say, "You must be the Anna Mae Bauer I've heard so much about," then lay down and died.

The Wisconsin Department of Natural Resources reports that more than 35,000 deer were killed by vehicles in one recent year—not all driven by Anna Mae Bauer. (If you're coming this way, the locals advise keeping the windows rolled down so the deer can jump right through.)

Trivia

Ellsworth is proud to be the "Cheese Curd Capital," but its cheese-makers are modest about this honor, saying that no one really makes cheese curds, they're just a by-product, scraps left over from an early stage of the cheddar-making process.

Ellsworth produces millions of pounds of cheese curds each year. They are not aged—the flavor "hasn't built up to a crescendo," a fact unrelated to the noise they make when eaten. Some people think cheese curds are peculiar, as if eating bland, rubbery little lumps that squeak is something to snicker at.

★ ★

Ghost Carriers in the Sky

Elk Mound

It is a little-known fact that Michael Feldman is the patron saint of rural letter carriers, or will be, once he is martyred. One particularly waggish carrier says that postal regulations actually require them to listen to *Whad'Ya Know* as they drive their routes, the better to know they are on schedule, since the Schultze place should come up just about the same time as the quiz in the first hour. If your mail is late on Saturday morning, it may well be because your carrier pulled over on Timber Road in Elk Mound and is attempting to answer the qualifying question on his cell phone.

It is only fitting, therefore, to make note of the unique memorial to the rural letter carriers of Dunn County: the Castle on Elk Mound Hill, elevation 1,207 feet. In 1934 rural letter carriers of Dunn County clambered to the top—it would be a few years before the WPA showed up with picks, shovels, and wheelbarrows to build a road—and placed a plaque dedicated to "the deceased rural letter carriers of Dunn County," planting a tree in soil taken from each carrier's route. These, after all, were the intrepid public servants who sallied forth in the days before you could wheel your own Taurus over class B highways, negotiating muddy and treacherous roads by horse and wagon in weather not fit for man nor beast.

Enter the WPA in 1938 to construct an impressive three-story hand-hewn stone tower, soon dubbed the Castle, the dominating landmark in these parts. At a dedication ceremony on Armistice Day that year, a roll call of deceased Dunn County letter carriers was forever sealed in the castle keep. Sightings of ghost carriers making their deliveries ensued; the Castle had been provided with a cookstove and dining room for their use, and for that of tourists attracted to the spot for its panoramic views of Dunn County, much like those the Chippewa had while scouting for elk and buffalo. Time and mischief have taken their toll on the Castle amenities, but the views remain spectacular, and some say enchanted by the ghost carriers in the sky above Elk Mound.

Today from the Castle you see herds of semis on I-94 racing to and from the Twin Cities.

Mound Hill Park, N435 Holly Avenue, is open from 8:00 a.m. to 10:00 p.m. daily, May through October. From the intersection of East Menomonie Street (Highway 12) and Holly Avenue in the village of Elk Mound, go north on Holly Avenue for a half mile to the park entrance on Elk Mound Hill Road. Take the winding road, posted 5 mph, to the top.

You're Cleared for Landing
Elmwood

Thousands of Earthlings, some in costume, come to Elmwood, population 775, for UFO Days in July.

The first reported sighting of a UFO here occurred in March 1975. Something like a very bright star chased a mother and her three children home and tried to land in front of their car. A few nights later, police officer George Wheeler sighted "a flaming ball the size of a football field." It zapped his car with a blue light that burned out all the plugs and points. The CIA investigated. Even Dan Rather came.

Enough sightings occurred over the next several years that in 1988 Elmwood announced plans for a $25 million visitor center—for aliens. It would include a gigantic beacon and landing strip, a huge image on the ground to welcome space travelers, accommodations and laboratories for dozens of scientists, and a video studio. "This is not a gimmick," said the mayor.

The ground image caused considerable debate. The sketch from a local artist showed two lanky figures shaking hands. What if a handshake doesn't mean the same thing to aliens that it means to humans? "If they're smart enough to get here," said the mayor, "they're smart enough to figure everything else out." The handshake stayed.

Elmwood dropped the plan for the visitor center for lack of funds, but it has an annual celebration on the last full weekend in July. There's a parade, dancing, sporting events, and, of course, UFO burgers and souvenirs. Call (715) 639-3792 for more information.

Yet another feather in Wisconsin's cap: the World's Largest Pine Log.

All Dressed Out and Nowhere to Go

Glidden

Here lies the "World Record Black Bear." It was killed 5 miles northeast of Glidden on November 23, 1963.

Hjalmer Krans had noticed a bear den while looking over a timber tract in a cedar swamp and reported his discovery to two hunters, Otto Hedbany and Donald Streubel of New Berlin. According to the *Glidden Enterprise,* "The bear had been denned for some time and did not bestir itself when discovered. Mr. Hedbany had no difficulty in killing the animal with one shot in the head, fired from his 303 Savage rifle. It took seven men about an hour to drag the bear 150 yards to a car."

The hunters weighed the bear at the Schraufnagel Lumber Yard: 665 pounds "dressed out." It measured 7 feet 10 inches from tail to nose and 72 inches around the chest, and it was estimated to be twelve years old.

The bear is in a display case at the intersection of Highway 13 and Grant Street. The world's largest white pine log (1,940 board feet) is 2 blocks east of Highway 13, just off Grant Street.

Paul Bunyan Just Got Better Press
Grantsburg

A life-size wood sculpture of a hometown hero, Anders Gustav Anderson (1872–1926), stands in front of the village office at 416 South Pine Street. "Big Gust" stood a well-proportioned 7 feet 6 inches (that's 4 inches taller than Kareem Abdul-Jabbar), weighed 360 pounds, and wore size 18 shoes (Kareem's are size 16).

Born in Sweden, Big Gust was village marshal of Grantsburg for the last twenty-five years of his life and the biggest police officer in the country. According to one story, Gust once broke up a disturbance at the local saloon by hoisting a man under each arm and heading toward the jail. At Oak and Madison they asked

Grantsburg didn't have a basketball team. COURTESY BURNETT COUNTY SENTINEL

to be put down and walked peaceably the rest of the way. He was also helpful if power lines needed to be strung or if a car or even a house needed to be lifted, for he was very strong.

Gust was also good-natured. When he died no one could recall an angry or unkind word from him; and if there were, chances are they would have let it pass.

Alf Manley Olson, a lifelong resident of Grantsburg, carved the Big Gust likeness in 1980 from laminated basswood. It weighs eight pounds more than Gust did. The Grantsburg Area Historical Society Museum, located at 133 West Wisconsin Avenue, displays the crutch specially built for Gust when he slipped on ice in front of the fire hall in 1918 and broke his hip, along with other items that indicate his size.

Grantsburg celebrates Big Gust Days the first weekend of June each year. For more information go to www.grantsburgwi.com/events.htm.

Fastest Show on H_2O

Grantsburg

What's the fun of having a snowmobile if you can zoom around in it only eight months out of the year? Some such thinking inspired the activity on Memory Lake that now attracts thousands of spectators every summer: drag races in snowmobiles on open water, something that usually happens only at bar time—Wisconsin parlance for "closing time"—when the ice is breaking up.

Three or four snowmobiles at a time take a 20-foot run from the shore, hit the water, and skip across the top, the way a rock skips across a pond. The fastest one wins—and speeds can reach 65 or 70 mph on the straightaway. Another event involves racing around a series of buoys. Whichever, unless it's done very fast, the snowmobile sinks.

The World Championship Snowmobile Watercross takes place on the third weekend in July and includes fireworks, music, and wrist-wrestling competitions. Call (715) 463-4269 for information.

The de rigueur photo op of your trip to northern Wisconsin, for not just you but up to twenty or thirty of your traveling companions—that's how big the jaws of this muskie are at the Fishing Hall of Fame. Big enough for weddings. WISCONSIN DEPARTMENT OF TOURISM

There's Always a Catch

Hayward

The Fresh Water Fishing Hall of Fame has hundreds of outboard motors from way back when ("Look! There's Grandpa's old motor!"), thousands of fishing poles and rods and reels, and more kinds of minnow buckets than you ever dreamed of. It's a trip down a memory lane of tackle boxes and depth finders. It's also the last word on freshwater fishing records. If you think you have a trophy, have it authenticated here.

But the part that made our hearts beat faster was the exhibit of hundreds of fishing hooks and lures that have snagged fishermen, each one documented by the angler's name, hometown (Illinois is well represented), and year and lake of snag. It began with the collection of a Grantsburg doctor who started to save the hooks and lures sticking out of people who turned up at his office about once a week for thirty-eight

What's Tall, Hairy, and Doesn't Wear a Packer Jersey?

Although Sasquatch—Bigfoot, to his friends—is most often associated with the Pacific Northwest, someone forgot to tell James Hughes of Granton, a deliveryman for the *Black River Shopper*. While on his route on Highway H at about 5:15 on the morning of March 28, 2000, Hughes saw a hirsute, ape-faced creature a good 8 feet tall and easily 500 pounds making off with a goat under one arm. Since the thing still had one arm free, Hughes put the pedal to the metal and left the *Shoppers* in his trunk. In his report to the Clark County Sheriff's Department, he described the beast as "all covered with hair, a real dark gray color, with some spots that look a honey color. It was walking on two legs, and it was mighty, mighty, big." Hughes feared for his life, but the creature had already gotten his goat. The sheriff, unable to find any footprints or scat, said he had no reports of goats missing, let alone, well, you know.

According to the *Milwaukee Journal Sentinel*, Hughes waited a day to file his report, fearing that people would think him crazy, but stressed, "I don't drink, I don't use dope, and I was wide awake."

summers. It didn't even have to be summertime; some folks hooked themselves cleaning out their tackle boxes in the middle of winter. Other doctors have joined in the fun to build the impressive collection on display here. (Howard Young Medical Center in Woodruff honors hook-and-lure victims with membership in the People Catchers Club.)

Also noteworthy is the wall of "Poor Taxidermy," the pathetic attempts of amateurs that resulted in misshapen fish or mounts that deteriorated from the use of inferior materials. With all the taxidermists

It would be easy to dismiss this report as an aberration were it not for the fact that Bigfoot sightings in Wisconsin have been numerous, dating from at least 1910, when a large, hairy creature followed a ten-year-old girl home, leaving tracks "twice as large as her father's." Before that a similar beast, the Windigo, was known to the Chippewa and incorporated into their tribal lore. In *The W-Files,* author Jay Rath recounts sightings of huge, upright, animal-like creatures in Delavan in 1964; in Waupaca County in 1968 (where a group of hunters would have shot it had it only looked a little less human); in Lafayette County in 1970; and in 1992 in southeastern Wisconsin, standing over a roadkill on Highway 106. More sightings of this last creature attracted national media, as well as tour buses from Illinois, and excited such alliterations as the Werewolf of Walworth County and *The Beast of Bray Road*, a book by Linda Godfrey.

All the descriptions are much the same as Hughes's. Needless to say, to see something of that size in Wisconsin without so much as a shred of Packer paraphernalia on it can only be described as very, very curious indeed.

Granton is in Clark County, about 10 miles east of Neillsville.

in business in the Northwoods, there's really no need to try this at home.

Did we mention that all these wonders are housed in a four-and-a-half-story, half-block-long, walk-through fiberglass muskie?

The National Fresh Water Fishing Hall of Fame is at the junction of Highways 27 and B. Open daily April 15 through October 31 from 9:30 a.m. to 4:30 p.m. in June, July, and August, to 4:00 p.m. at other times. For more information visit www.freshwater-fishing.org or call (715) 634-4440.

★ ★

Trivia

Dick's Bar in Hudson serves chicken in a hubcap with soup or salad on the side. Those who must know why are told of a dream involving chickens and hubcaps, "and if you understand that, we've failed." No need to count your hubcaps before you drive away.

Dick's has been in the same location since 1860: next to the marina on the Mississippi River, 111 Walnut Street (old Highway 12). Open 8:00 a.m. to bar time. Give them a call at (715) 386-5222.

Pull Up Your Galluses and Head for the Timber
Hayward

If you've always worn red flannels and suspenders and searched in vain for like-minded individuals, you'll want to add to the cries of "Yo-ho!" at the Lumberjack World Championships. Lumberjacks and lumberjills come from all over the world to compete in such events as the spring-board chop, hot saw, underhand chop, logrolling, boom run, and speed climb.

Muscular competitors climb up and down trees about 90 feet tall very, very fast. They saw through logs in a wink. They spin big logs underfoot while trying to dump each other into the water. They toss axes all over the place. In short, it's a lot like where you work, only out-doors. Today, of course, all these things are usually done by machine (the logroller can dump a guy in the drink in a split second), so it's a glimpse of life in the Northwoods in days gone by.

This big event, along with other activities and music, takes place on the last full weekend in July at Lumberjack Bowl, a quarter mile east of Hayward on Highway B. For more information call (715) 634-2484 or go to www.lumberjackworldchampionships.com.

P.S. Galluses are suspenders.

To Taxidermy
Hayward

The trouble with most dead things is they don't make you laugh. But that is easily remedied in Hayward at the whimsical Moccasin Bar, which features better drinking through taxidermy.

We're talking more than your usual fetal deer tableau here. We're talking rabbits in calico kibitzing at sheepshead and Tyrolean-hatted chipmunks drinking beer and rolling dice. Things that would have been, had evolution favored rodents and other small mammals instead of us. See what might have been at this popular local hangout.

Some folks come just to see the "World's Largest Muskie"—largest *mounted* muskie, that is—(67½ pounds and 60¼ inches) caught by Cal Johnson on July 24, 1949. In 2005, however, the World Record Muskie Alliance begged to differ and challenged the claim in a deeply serious ninety-five-page report documented with forensic imaging and pixelated proof. So life giveth and it taketh away.

Horsepower!

Huntsinger Farms of Eau Claire is the world's largest grower and processor of horseradish.

★ ★

Judge Wolf hears the case of the badger that jumped the woodcock season at the Moccasin Bar in Hayward.

The Moccasin Bar is at the junction of Highways 63 and 27. Open 9:00 a.m. to bar time daily. Call (715) 634-4211.

Mark Twine
Lake Nebagamon

James Frank Kotera (aka JFK) has a mighty big ball of twine. He started it in 1979, after reading about other twine balls around the country. There are quite a few of them, though nobody knows why. Maybe because they are less painful to collect than balls of barbed wire.

From the beginning Jim has kept track of the size of his ball—"I take a whole bunch of twine, put it in a garbage bag, and weigh the garbage bag"—and according to his records, the twine ball now weighs 19,722 pounds. That's assuming a twine ball wound weighs the same as a twine ball unwound. Along the way he's marked it on

Can You Say Chequamegon?

Not a day goes by in Wisconsin that somebody doesn't mangle the word Oconomowoc. Or Weyauwega. Or the names of many other towns, lakes, Indian tribes, forests, or prominent people around the state. Butte des Morts. Lac Courtes Oreilles. Shawano. Ashwaubenon. Rio. Former Packer quarterback Bret Favre (never mind the way it's spelled). Kabeer Gbaja-Biamila. But there's "a halfway decent resource for learning to pronounce stuff in Wisconsin," says Jackie Johnson, the creator of MissPronouncer.com, an online guide with audio for all things Wisconsin. In some cases the very subject does the pronouncing. After all, who would know better how to pronounce their own names than Madison mayor Dave Cieslewicz or supreme court chief justice Shirley Abrahamson? "And by the way," says Jackie, "please slap anyone who says WESconsin!" That address is www.misspronouncer.com.

door jambs like a toddler. Today it's all growed up: almost 8 feet tall, 35 feet across, and potato shaped, since Jim has to work the angles now that it's too big to roll.

If his calculations are correct (and unless someone has a ten-ton twine ball hidden away somewhere), he has the largest twine ball assembled by one man. There's one in Darwin, Minnesota, but it weighs a mere 17,400 pounds and measures 12 feet (Darwinians nevertheless hold an annual festival called Twine Ball Days in August). And there's one that the Ripley's Believe It or Not Museum in Branson, Missouri, flaunts as Guinness-record-size, but it was a group effort, as was

★ ★

JFK's twine ball.

the 11-footer in Cawker City, Kansas (which calls its August celebration Twine-a-thon).

A farmer in the neighborhood has supplied much of the twine, and now he can't find anything to bundle his papers with. Meanwhile, Jim built a pole shed over the ball to protect it from winter weather and even assembled a forty-seven-pound demo ball to show visitors how it's done. The address is 8009 South Oakdale Road (at Minnesuing Road), in the town of Highland, near Lake Nebagamon. Once you find the Oakdale Road–Minnesuing Road intersection, it will be the giant potato-shaped twine ball on the left. Call (715) 374-3518 for more information.

In a Blizzard, Of Course, You Could Actually Be Driving Up Christmas Trees
Madeline Island

Highway H in Bayfield County is 2.5 miles longer in winter than the rest of the year. That's because it extends to Madeline Island from Bayfield when Chequamegon Bay freezes over—usually in January. Regular ferry service ends, and all kinds of other transportation begin. Say you live on the island and want to get to Bayfield; you have your choice of snowmobile, van, car, or windsled (a vehicle that combines boat, plane, and sled). Or, if you want to know what it would be like to live on Mars, you could walk. Your choice depends on the condition of the ice.

Your route is a road of ice that is plowed, outlined in Christmas trees, and maintained until the ice starts to thaw, usually in March or April. Car-shaped holes in the ice indicate that the ice-road season is over. *Whatever*

The Nelson brothers' windsled transports schoolchildren, commuters, groceries, and library books. WISCONSIN DEPARTMENT OF TOURISM

★ ★

you do, don't go out on that ice without first calling Arnie and Ronnie Nelson. They know the ice and have maintained the road for years. Visit Windsleds, Inc., at www.windsled.com or call (715) 747-5400.

Where There's Smokey
Mercer

Until 1950 Smokey Bear existed only on paper—in posters and advertisements of the USDA Forest Service. But that was before the rangers at the station in Mercer needed an idea for a parade float for the Fireman's Convention in Hurley in August. Inspired by a recent Smokey Bear poster, their float featured a bearskin-and-wood Smokey praying under the sign with the words PLEASE MAKE PEOPLE CAREFUL. AMEN.

Smokey reappeared the following month at the Logging Congress parade in Wausau, this time in the form of a ranger wearing a bear costume. Smokey Bear personified was a big hit!

The idea spread like wildfire, and before long the Forest Service was suiting up lots of Smokeys. Today the Wisconsin Department of Natural Resources is officially credited with fabricating the first Smokey Bear costume.

The nation's first Smokey Bear head is at the ranger station in Mercer.
PATTI BROWN, DNR

Moving Is Never Easy

The old-timers had doubts about the wisdom of moving a house across the ice, but the movers (from Minneapolis) said they'd checked it—2 feet thick all the way across. The furnished seven-room, two-story house and trailer (twenty tons) were to be towed from Port Superior to Madeline Island on a truck (ten tons), a distance of slightly more than 3 miles. The ice-wise shook their heads.

On March 2, 1977, the thirty-ton cavalcade set out across the ice. Things went well most of the way, but then, just a mile from Madeline Island, the wheels under the house dropped through on one side, and the "Spectacle on Ice" came to a full halt. From the shore the gallery watched the house slowly settle into the water and disappear.

"The only thing sticking up was the chimney of the fireplace," recalls Ed Erickson, a veteran of these waters. "We filled the chimney with sandbags and that didn't go, so then we hauled rock and set rocks on the eaves, and it settled to the bottom of the lake."

In the spring Ed tried to lift the house, but it fell apart. He hauled up the pieces, but the floor is still down there.

The head of the original costume is at the Mercer-area ranger station. Conservation aide Frank Brunner Jr. created it, and years later forestry technician Dave Sleight rescued it from a warehouse. A good collection of vintage posters is on display, too. Smokey's keeper is head ranger Tim Fitzgerald, and his station is a half mile north of town, on State House Road. Open 8:00 a.m. to 4:30 p.m. Mondays and Fridays or by appointment. Call (715) 476-2240 for more information.

★ ★

Trivia

Smokey Bear appears in the Fourth of July parade and at Mercer's annual Loon Day in August. (Well, actually, it's the official USDA Forest Service costume—in accordance with the Smokey Bear Act of 1952, Public Law 82-359—containing a human and a NASA-worthy cooling system so Smokey doesn't pass out.) Loon Day includes loon-calling contests.

Largest Talking Cow and Cheese Replica
Neillsville

Chatty Belle is the world's largest talking cow, and . . . but drop a quarter in the slot and let her tell the story: "Hi, so nice to see you. My name is Chatty Belle. What's your name? [pause] Well, nice to meet you. Did you know I'm the world's largest talking cow? I'm 16 feet high at the shoulders and 20 feet long, seven times as large as the average Holstein." Her voice seems high for such a large cow.

Until 2005, Chatty Belle shared this spot with a semitrailer containing the world's largest cheese replica, a polystyrene version of the 35,000-pound cheddar that Wisconsin proudly exhibited at the 1964–65 New York World's Fair. Picture 16,000 cows in single file, stretching down the road for 20 miles—that's the size of the herd that gave the milk that made the cheese that went to the fair.

But the cheesemobile deteriorated over the years, and now Chatty Belle stands alone, facing Highway 10 on the east edge of town, next to the Wisconsin pavilion—which, as Chatty Belle explains, represented the state at the World's Fair. It houses WCCN-AM, and it looks like a party hat with an antenna on top.

Wood Tick Capital of the World
Oxbo

Louisville has the Kentucky Derby, Indianapolis has the Indy 500, and Oxbo has the annual wood tick race, a strange little insect derby that began in 1979. Each spring hundreds of people join the ten residents of Oxbo for a race that takes place in a tent next to the Oxbo Resort, your basic knotty pine tavern with a couple of heads on the wall and a few cans of Dinty Moore and Sterno on the shelf.

Two contestants at a time take their ticks to the racing table and release them from their little tick carriers (aspirin tins, film canisters, lockets) onto the center of a bull's-eye target. The ticks wander around, and the first tick out of the bull's-eye is the winner of the heat. The mayor of Oxbo smashes the losing tick with a gavel, to ensure that losing-tick genes are not bred again. None of them goes to stud. It's a sad fate, considering the past year of workouts, lifting little weights and running on tiny treadmills.

The competition continues until only two ticks remain. The one that survives the championship heat wins a cash prize, a trophy, and a place in the Wood Tick Hall of Fame.

"We have a lot of fun doing something incredibly stupid," says one of the regulars.

The event is held on a Saturday afternoon in May. Located just off Highway 70 at the Flambeau River, 15 miles west of Park Falls. Call (715) 762-4786 for details or go to www.oxboresort.com.

Wisconsin Concrete Park
Phillips

Of all the Wisconsin folks who toted bags of cement for their art, Fred Smith was one of the most prolific. In this Northwoods town he created more than 200 huge figures of animals and people: moose, fish, lions, owls, pioneers, soldiers, angels, kings, and queens. For features and other details he used insulator knobs and pieces of brown beer bottles and bleach bottles and blue Mason jars.

★ ★

Fred Smith remembered friends, local history, and folklore at his Concrete Park in Phillips. WISCONSIN DEPARTMENT OF TOURISM (DOUG ALFT)

Fred's figures don't just stand there like statues. They're drinking beer, celebrating a double wedding, riding around on horses. The output is amazing for one person, especially considering that Fred didn't get started until age sixty-three. People thought Fred had really gone round the bend when, in about 1950, this fantastical world began to appear in the pine grove next to his Rock Garden Tavern.

Cutting to the chase of the creative urge, Fred confessed, "Nobody knows why I made them. Not even me. The work just came to me naturally."

Fred's place was always a lively gathering spot. The dances and musical events that took place in his barn were legendary, with Fred playing fiddle or mandolin and keeping time with bells strapped to his legs.

Concrete Park, open year-round during daylight hours, is located on the southern edge of Phillips on Highway 13. No admission is charged, but, as Fred used to say, "Donations appreciated." For more information call (800) 269-4505 or visit www.friendsoffredsmith.org. Guided tours for groups can be arranged.

From Young Shavers Mighty Carvers Grow
Shell Lake

Joseph Barta (1904–1972) was a high school math teacher and basketball coach who, for some reason that he could not explain, had wanted to carve the Last Supper since he was sixteen. He'd started carving—"whittling," his family called it—when he was ten.

His family wasn't especially encouraging, either. "You'll cut yourself, Joe," his mother warned. "I'm tired of cleaning up your mess of shavings," his sister complained. Joe wasn't even a churchgoer, yet the compulsion to carve the monumental piece became almost consuming.

By the time Barta was in his forties, he had left teaching to carve full-time. The Museum of Woodcarving in

Joe Barta's Judas.

Continued on Page 44

Urban and Rural Wisconsin Legends

1. Cows—how much should you tip? Cow tipping (the pushing over of a sleeping cow by bored adolescent farm youths before they get the keys to the pickup) appears to occur, along with flicking your Bic on cows' methane emissions and putting the odd goose egg under the odd hen. The domino effect—collapsing an entire chorus line of cows—has never been documented. Two good-size youths working in concert can provide a Holstein with a thrill she'll never forget. One tip: Make sure you push from the uphill side.

2. The cow with the porthole. Since we're on the subject, yes, there is a cow with a porthole (several in fact) in the dairy barns at the University of Wisconsin in Madison. The device allows access to the fascinating rumens of the ruminates, which gives animal husbanders something to think about (if cows had as many brains as stomachs, they'd be Einsteins instead of Holsteins). Having actually seen a cow with the window of opportunity, I will tell you that I was somewhat disappointed; it was not like the access on a front-loading dryer, and you couldn't see anything going around inside.

   By the by, the university is working on genetic designer milks by milking white mice. How do they do it? Tiny little stools.

3. Sasquatch summers in Wisconsin. A large (if you consider 7 feet tall large), hairy, manlike creature has been sighted numerous times in northern Wisconsin, although most times it turns out to be a large, hairy man. But not always. In 1992 an oversize hirsute primate with a skunklike odor was spotted alongside a Jefferson County highway, standing over a road-killed raccoon, apparently deciding how to prepare it. The sighting, however, was by two guys from Illinois who simply may not be used to folks up here.

(Frankly, we've seen worse in Chicago, and with pinky rings.)

4. There are Socialists in the sewers of Milwaukee. Wrong. The Socialists built the sewers of Milwaukee, one of their most fundamental contributions. Milwaukee had many Socialist politicians and mayors, until we discovered they were National Socialists.

5. The Virgin Mary has appeared in a bathtub in Kenosha. True— in fact, in many bathtubs, the backyard bathtub grotto being endemic to Kenosha and Racine Counties, where religious and handy Sicilian immigrants, putting in showers during bathroom remodels, stuck the old tubs on end in their backyards with the Virgin standing in them. Some of them are quite elaborate, with masonry, lights, and, yes, running water. Head out Highway 50 and peek into a lot of backyards.

6. An intact flying saucer landed and until recently was preserved in Appleton, Wisconsin. A case of mistaken identity—that round,

Continued on Page 42

Bathtub grottoes. JIM LEGAULT

Lease Day junk.

futuristic structure with the rotating lights was actually the Aid Association for Lutherans, the place for all your Lutheran insurance needs. Wisconsin has had its share of sightings, abductions, and ignition points on squad cars ruined by interference from alien craft, although most are thought to be from Highland Park, Illinois. Elmwood considered building a landing strip and beacon for extraterrestrial craft, so there you go.

7. If you attended the University of Wisconsin–Madison within the past forty years or so, your furniture is still here. True. On August 15, when all the twelve-month apartment leases expire, recent graduates pile up their furniture on the curb and drive away to Milwaukee or Minneapolis or Mequon to start their new lives. Incoming students, whose leases begin on August 16, haul the abandoned furniture away to their new apartments, before the city trucks have time to pick it up. When those students graduate, they dump their furniture on the curb, and newcomers retrieve it, ad infinitum. Thus, through the annual ritual known as Lease Day, end tables, plaid Herculon couches, and TV stands from the 1960s are still in use today.

8. Official NFL gear in Green Bay includes green-and-gold caskets. Well, maybe not official, but true. Fred Angermann of Wisconsin Vault and Casket designed and makes the caskets, which, not being officially sanctioned by the Packers, do not bear the logo, although the overall effect is unmistakable. More than thirty have been sold so far, several have been interred, and others turn up at tailgate parties at Lambeau Field. It seems only fitting, since your only hope at season tickets is in the next lifetime.

9. Wisconsin emits strange radio frequencies. It's true. And a lot of it has to do with the U.S. Navy. In fact, the claim for the first radio broadcast of any kind is held by a Navy project. In 1917 station 9XM in Madison broadcast exotic AM waves to ships at sea and held on to become the nation's first public radio station, WHA (by chance, the home of *Michael Feldman's Whad'Ya Know?*).

   Not content with this early success, in the 1980s the Navy constructed a huge and controversial low-frequency antenna that is buried in a giant oval beneath thousands of acres of northern Wisconsin woods. Known alternately as "Project ELF" (for "extremely low frequency") or "Sanguine," it is designed to communicate with submerged nuclear submarines during time of war should everything topside be, shall we say, inoperative. In the event of a third and final world war, the signal to launch will come from us.

10. Without Wisconsin, there would be no rock 'n' roll. Well, without Wisconsin's Les Paul, there would be no rock 'n' roll as we know it. Working in his garage in West Allis in 1941, Paul attached a string to a railroad tie and came up with the prototype for the solid-body electric guitar, without which Chuck Berry, Jimmy Page, Pete Townshend, and Frank Zappa would not have been possible. Les Paul's first working model was, in fact, dubbed "the log," and later metamorphosed into the beautiful Les Paul Gibson. The solid-body electric guitar allowed sustain and distortion, and if you have sustain and distortion, you have rock 'n' roll.

★ ★

Shell Lake shows what happened after that. The collection includes hundreds of miniatures (prehistoric creatures; every variety of cow, dog, and woodland animal; JFK on a campaign swing through Spooner) and a hundred life-size re-creations, most of them biblical figures—not only the 26-foot-long Last Supper (representing four years of carving), but also Christ from nativity to crucifixion, as well as Daniel in the lions' den. One of the lions looks like Joseph Stalin; elsewhere, Herod, from the New Testament, looks like Adolf Eichmann. A coincidence?

The Barta woodcarving collection—the largest created by one man—was exhibited at the Disney Epcot Center for two years, but now it is back in northern Wisconsin, where it grew. The collection is on Highway 63 just north of Shell Lake. Open daily 9:00 a.m. to 6:00 p.m. May through October. Call (715) 468-7100 for details.

Where Guys Keep Scratching "JFK" above the Urinal
Spooner

The Buckhorn Bar in Spooner is festooned with taxidermy, as are many taverns in the area. But particularly noteworthy here are the two-headed calf and the plaques on the door of the men's room: JOHN F. KENNEDY USED THESE FACILITIES ON MARCH 18, 1960 and GOVERNOR TOMMY G. THOMPSON USED THESE FACILITIES ON MAY 3, 1997.

Senator Kennedy had stopped in to shake hands after a campaign speech outside on the main street of Spooner. He didn't finish the beer someone bought him, but he did use the men's room before returning to the campaign trail. It is not known whether he washed his hands afterward, since he was not an employee.

Grasping the historic significance of these acts under the roof of the Buckhorn that day, the owner enshrined the beer glass in a special case and ordered a plaque for the door. He checked the men's room as well, but saw nothing of museum quality. Thirty-seven years rolled by, and, don't you know, Wisconsin governor Tommy Thompson drops in one day with some fishing buddies, empties a beer glass, and visits the men's room. And—his secretary was named Kennedy. The plaque in his honor appeared not long afterward.

The Buckhorn is on the corner at 105 Walnut, a block east of Highway 53 on the main business street of Spooner. It also has a beautiful wood-and-glass backbar that the Leinenkugel Brewery installed in the 1930s. For more information call (715) 635-6008.

2

Northeast

The Northwoods, in *the upper part of northeast Wisconsin, has a lot of lakes and loons, and its people know how to have a good time. They put costumes on beef roasts and parade them down the street. They wear snowshoes to play baseball.*

But the northeast has its serious side. It is the home of world leaders in the manufacture of sauerkraut, toilet seats, and manhole covers. And scattered throughout this part of Wisconsin are champions of all kinds—men who excel at eating bratwurst and Big Macs, champions (at times) of professional football, and a cow named Lucinda who, year after year, gives more milk than any other cow in the world.

As if all this were not enough, at a certain spot in northeast Wisconsin you can stand at the exact center of the northern half of the Western Hemisphere. You'd have to go halfway around the world for another 45- x 90-degree opportunity like that. Maybe Henry David Thoreau wouldn't have gone "'round the world to count the cats in Zanzibar," but if he'd been near Poniatowski, even he might have sought out this unique geographic spot. So could you.

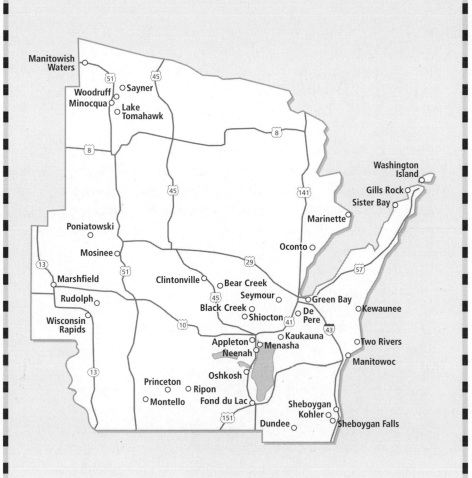

Manitowish
Waters

⑤51   ㊸45

Woodruff   ○ Sayner
Minocqua   ○ Lake
           Tomahawk

⑧8

⑧8

㊸45

⑧8

141

Washington
Island

Gills Rock ○
Sister Bay ○

Marinette

Poniatowski
○

Mosinee ○

Oconto ○

13

Marshfield ○

51

Clintonville ○   Bear Creek ○

29

57

Rudolph ○

㊸45   Seymour ○

Green Bay

Kewaunee ○

Black Creek   Shiocton ○
De
Pere

Wisconsin
Rapids

10

41

43

Appleton ○   Kaukauna ○
Neenah   Menasha

Two Rivers ○

13

Oshkosh ○

Manitowoc

Princeton
○   Ripon ○

○ Montello

Fond du Lac ○

151

Dundee ○

Sheboygan ○
Kohler ○
Sheboygan Falls ○

Northeast

★ ★

Houdini: Got Milk?
Appleton

Being the son of a rabbi, perhaps Harry Houdini's greatest escape was not going to the yeshiva and finding himself a nice little congregation in Appleton. But Harry could wriggle out of rolltop desks, piano cases, coffins, and steamer trunks. Even tossing some such thing into the river—with Houdini in it—was not too much to ask of the greatest escape artist who ever lived.

In one famous trick, Houdini told the audience to take a deep breath, took one himself, and then disappeared into a sixty-gallon milk can filled with water. Assistants sealed the can shut. Onstage a clock ticked away . . . and away . . . and away. No sign of Houdini. People

Sculptor Richard C. Wolter signed the lock on *Metamorphosis* "Best wishes, Houdini." It's on a plaza just south of College Avenue, near the intersection with Appleton Street. A marker nearby notes that Houdini was "a high-spirited and troublesome little boy who one night unlocked the front-door locks of all the merchants on College Avenue."

started to panic and take off, leaving him to reappear to a greatly diminished house.

More of Houdini's amazing deeds are revealed in an interactive exhibit at the History Museum, along with artifacts related to his life and career.

Houdini spent several idyllic childhood years in Appleton and called it his hometown, although he was born in Hungary. (He died in Detroit of peritonitis, the Tony Curtis movie version of his life notwithstanding.) Houdini's boyhood home and the spot on the Fox River where he nearly drowned are among fifteen locations on a Houdini walking-tour map available at the museum. It explains the presence, elsewhere in Appleton, of the Houdini Lounge, Houdini Elementary School, and Houdini Square.

The Houdini exhibit is at the History Museum at the Castle, 330 East College Avenue. The museum also has an Edna Ferber exhibit and walking-tour map. The Ferber and Houdini maps both show where Appleton's favorite daughter interviewed its favorite son for the *Crescent* in 1904. Open 10:00 a.m. to 4:00 p.m. Tuesday through Saturday (and Monday between Memorial Day and Labor Day), noon to 4:00 p.m. Sunday. Admission charge. For more information call (920) 735-9370 or visit www.myhistorymuseum.org/houdini.

The Measure of a Man
Black Creek

A few miles south of Black Creek, along Highway 47, are hand-lettered signs that shout not about the Apocalypse, not about gun control, but about a humble unit of measurement: the inch.

Some years ago, when he worked as a carpenter, James Franklin Brunette determined that what the United States Bureau of Standards is trying to pass off as the inch is actually 0.9375 of that amount. (Anyone who has ever bought a two-by-four would tend to agree.)

Beyond Brunette's driveway and scattered throughout his property are many exhibits that demonstrate his intriguing proposition. Wheels

Magnifico proves his point . . .

and contrivances are covered with millions of numbers, painstakingly hand-painted in primary colors to six decimal places, to compare and show the progression of German millimeters, English millimeters, and our joke of a U.S. inch. The most elaborate exhibit is his Stonehenge, a huge circle of stones and flags and bags that proves the folly of taking the Bureau of Standards at its word.

Brunette, aka "Magnifico the Math Master, Arithmetician Extraordinaire," is concerned about the ramifications of it all, for everything from dot-matrix printers to highway safety. He holds forth on the subject at his J. F. B. Art and Math Museum, 5107 Highway 47, south of Black Creek. You can reach him at (920) 739-0733.

Is That a Great Wall or What?
Clintonville

Four-wheel-drive technology was developed here early in the twentieth century, and in the 1920s Walter Olen and the Four Wheel Drive Corporation's heavy-duty trucks traveled far and wide. They helped build

The Great Wall of China at Clintonville. ERICA SCHLUETER

★ ★

railways in China, a project that led to Olen's hauling home a hefty
souvenir: a portion of the Great Wall of China, which, to date, has pro-
tected Clintonville from possible invaders from the north. A gift from
revered statesman Sun Yatsen, it is believed to be the only section of
the Great Wall ever to leave China.

Eventually Olen's 1,700-year-old Chinese bricks were joined by stones
from such places as Jerusalem, the Petrified Forest, Yellowstone National
Park, and the Dakota Badlands, along with a Wisconsin millstone. The
exotic mementos are lined up in Pioneer Park on the banks of the
Pigeon River (where huge flocks of pigeons used to roost in the trees)
near two historic houses and the Four Wheel Drive Museum, which displays original four-wheel-drive vehicles—a must-visit for SUVs or urban
assault vehicles seeking to return to their roots. The museum is open by
appointment only. To arrange tours, call (715) 823-2141, ext. 1209.

What's Green and Gold and Leaps
Tall Grandstands?
Green Bay

As you approach the Green Bay Packers Hall of Fame in Titletown
U.S.A., the landscape grows more green-and-gold. Even the lawn
ornaments wear Packer shirts in the team colors. This is the home of
the only major-league professional team owned by its fans, 57,000 of
whom are on its legendary waiting list for season tickets.

The intense bond between the Packers and their fans became even
more apparent when the museum reopened with the $295 million ren-
ovation of Lambeau Field in 2003. Invited to contribute memorabilia to
a room called Titletown's Finest, fans responded in a big way by send-
ing in their treasures. From this embarrassment of riches were selected
such items as license plates, a retainer with a Packers *G* made by an
orthodontist, a photograph of someone's pet cat in a Packer uniform,
and even one of Ray Nitschke's old cigar butts. After months of debate
and meditation ("I even prayed about it"), one fan finally parted with a
pair of coach Vince Lombardi's shoes.

The Lost Dauphin

In De Pere's Lost Dauphin Park there was once a humble log cabin that was thought to have housed the rightful pretender to the throne of France, Prince Louis XVII. He was known in these parts as Eleazer Williams. What distinguished Williams from the average Badger claiming royal descent was the fact that he was a French child who had been placed among the Iroquois Indians of New York at about the time of the dauphin's death/disappearance in the Temple in Paris, where his parents and sister were also imprisoned. If the story was to be believed, the sickly dauphin was smuggled out of Paris by his jailer Simon, and with the help of former servants, he was transported to the New World and placed among the St. Regis band in New York.

As a missionary and liaison to the Oneida tribe, Williams emigrated with them to Wisconsin in 1821 and became an influential leader—seeking, some said, to establish an Indian kingdom under his rule. His Bourbon origins were apparently unknown to him until a visit made to Green Bay in 1841 by Prince de Joinville, son of King Louis-Philippe. In one of the stranger evenings at the Astor Hotel, the prince informed Williams that he was indeed the son of Louis XVI and Marie Antoinette, and offered him a considerable estate if he would renounce all claims to the French throne.

None of us around here was born yesterday, and Williams was no different: He refused to sign and held out for a better deal. Unfortunately, that never came, and he eventually died penniless in his little cabin in the woods.

While the Reverend Williams never assumed the throne of France, it is a fact that for many years following his death, scores of Oneida children were named Eleazer. Visitors can climb the hillside in the park off Highway D (Lost Dauphin Road), just north of Little Rapids Road, and take in the Fox River—the beautiful domain of the "Lost Dauphin."

★ ★

At tailgate parties outside Lambeau Field, cheeseheads line up to be photographed with Saint Vince and his guardian angel (John O'Neill and Mary Beth Johnson of Cross Plains). The money goes to charity. ANDY KRAUSHAAR

The shoes ended up in Lombardi's locker in the display that recognizes the twenty-one Packers in the Pro Football Hall of Fame. Other special exhibits include a re-creation of Lombardi's office (you can even sit at his desk), a slab of concrete from the original tunnel that players used to enter and exit the playing grounds, a diorama of the 1967 Ice Bowl, a padded wall where fans can make their own Lambeau Leap (the touchdown celebration in which the scoring player leaps into the arms of fans in the stands), and, last but not least, the three Super Bowl trophies in a room so ethereal that, says one Packer official, "it's almost like you're in church." Many plaques, artifacts, videos, and interactive exhibits round out the 25,000-square-foot museum, the first to celebrate a single professional football team.

★ ★

The Packers Hall of Fame, 1265 Lombardi Avenue (1.3 miles east of Highway 41 from exit 167), is located in the lower level of the Lambeau Field atrium. Open 9:00 a.m. to 6:00 p.m. daily on nongame days. Admission charge. See www.lambeaufield.com for hours on game days, which vary according to kickoff time, and on holidays, or call (920) 569-7512 or (888) 442-7225.

Gutzon Borglum Would Be So Proud
Kaukauna

Florence has Michelangelo, the Iowa State Fair has the Butter Cow Lady, and Wisconsin has Troy Landwehr, cheese carver to the stars. His magnum opus is a 30-by-30-inch Mount Rushmore carved from a 700-pound block of cheddar, but he has also rendered TV and sports personalities. Mount Rushmore was commissioned by Cheez-It crackers

The big cheese and Troy pose in Times Square. RAY STUBBLEBINE

★ ★

A French fry purchased at Culver's in Wisconsin Rapids in June 2003 was listed as the world's largest french fry on the Internet auction site eBay. It measured 6¾ inches and sold for $202.50.

and, after its unveiling in New York City in 2007, it toured ten cities in a refrigerated bus with windows.

Troy got started at age eleven when Little Chute's Great Wisconsin Cheese Festival recruited the 4-H Club for a cheese carver. One lesson was all it took for Troy to get invited to that year's festival, and every year after that. Later he earned a BFA in graphic art at the Milwaukee Institute of Art and Design and was in signage for a while, but the phone kept ringing—they wanted cheese logos, bald eagles, cows, wedding bells, Republican elephants, and Democrat donkeys. He favors cheddar for its oils and consistency and carves with clay tools and piano wire.

The rest of the time Troy is a vintner, proprietor of Kerrigan Brothers Winery, N2797 Highway 55, 3 miles north of Kaukauna (exit 148 off Highway 41). The name Kerrigan honors his grandmother's five brothers, who would have relished a visit here. Call (920) 788-1423 or visit www.kerriganbrothers.com.

"Just Send Our Ma-ail . . ."
Kewaunee

"The Kewaunee Jail" was never a hit for the Kingston Trio, but it might have been, Kewaunee's having a leg up on Tijuana's, that being the leg an inmate removed from a bathtub to bop the jailer in a successful escape. Personally, I'd like to know what the guy was in for who carved a brass key from the water faucet to make his exit.

The Kewaunee slammer.

★ ★

Showers are the rule these days, but you can still see the three-legged bathtub in what is now a jail museum, along with the dungeon-type cells with their antique skeleton locks, the cots, tin cups, and shackles, which portray a (perhaps too) vivid diorama of the county accommodations in Kewaunee circa 1880. No room with a view, this one, all part of the punishment since the jailhouse stands like a blind lighthouse over the Lake Michigan harbor of this picturesque town.

The sheriff here ran a tight ship. Among the rules: "Prisoners must not deface walls by writing, scratching, or by pasting pictures of any kind on walls or in the cells. Penalty for violation: bread and water diet." No loud talking, no phone calls, no kangaroo courts (another cause for bread and water)—man, it was like a jail in there! In 1969 the inmates (or their descendents) were relocated to the euphemistic new Safety Building next door, and today the lockup just serves inmate ghosts with three strikes, possibly four, against them.

In the cells where Kewaunee County's scoundrels weren't allowed to spit ("Any prisoner spitting on walls, floors, ceilings, or defacing same, in any manner, will be placed in solitary confinement"), tourists of a certain type drool over Raggedy Anns, a tiny tea set, cattle ear-tag pliers, ox shoes, gauntlet gloves for logging, photos of guys with handlebar mustaches and a threshing crew in overalls, women beaming over their new-fangled washing machines, Gordy Reckelberg's music stand, and other non sequiturs. Well, life on the inside just wasn't that interesting.

Just for good measure, the county has provided nineteenth-century medical, clerical, agricultural, and tax records to put the jail experience in context. The pièce de résistance of the museum is a massive, very nearly full-scale carving of Custer's Last Stand. For reasons unknown, two local men dedicated about six years of their spare time—evenings, holidays, weekends—to capturing the details of the Battle of the Little Bighorn in 30 square feet of basswood. Custer's Stand alone is worth the trip, if not the incarceration.

The Kewaunee County Historical Museum is at Vliet and Dodge Streets. Open Memorial Day through Labor Day, noon to 4:30 p.m.,

off-season by appointment. Call (920) 388-3858 or visit www.roots
web.com/~wikchs for more information.

Take the Plunge
Kohler

John Michael Kohler got into the plumbing business in 1883, when
he enameled the inside of a dual-purpose horse trough/hog scalder,
attached four legs, and sold it to a farmer as a bathtub. Little did he
know what he had set in motion.

Today the bathroom products of Kohler Co. are admired near and
far. Kohler Co. has artist-edition sinks that are embellished with moss
roses and tell fairy tales ("Once upon a time a youth was enamored of
a beautiful girl but a frog cast a spell . . ."), or that depict panoramas
of Kohler's PGA-worthy Whistling Straits golf course.

A museum at the Kohler Design Center traces the evolution of
plumbing fixtures from hog scalder to the Provincial line, with its
country meadow of rabbits, birds, and flowers. Original pieces tell the
story—zoned bathrooms of the 1940s and 1950s had separate areas
for each activity and triggered the master-bedroom suite; gracious-
living bathrooms of the 1980s with whirlpool baths and fine furniture
introduced sensory appeal.

Across the street, free guided "Industry in Action" factory tours
walk visitors through the manufacturing process, from the unbaked
gray clay to today's ever-popular white, colored, or embellished toilet,
sink, or tub. The three-hour tours begin at 8:30 a.m. Monday through
Friday. Call (920) 457-3699 to sign up. The Kohler Design Center, 101
Upper Road, is open 8:00 a.m. to 5:00 p.m. Monday through Friday,
10:00 a.m. to 4:00 p.m. Saturday and Sunday. You will never look at
your toilet the same way again.

The Great Wall of China at Kohler. WISCONSIN DEPARTMENT OF TOURISM

★ ★

Trivia

The American Club in Kohler, today a luxurious five-diamond resort hotel, was originally built to house immigrant workers. There, after a long, hard day at the plumbing fixtures factory, they could relax in its reading rooms, card and billiard rooms, bar, and four-lane bowling alley.

46-Inch Shoes with Spikes
Lake Tomahawk

For people, unlike myself, who've never had the experience of walking around in 46-inch-long shoes, Lake Tomahawk offers a novel form of sport—baseball on snowshoes. Imagine going for a ground ball with contraptions that measure 12 inches wide and nearly 4 feet long attached to your feet! Imagine sliding into second! The 16-inch ball doesn't necessarily make it easier. No wonder Lake Tomahawk, home of the Snow Hawks, can safely proclaim itself Snowshoe Baseball Capital of the World.

On the other hand, go to a game and you soon see the appeal. For one thing, the players arrive swinging six-packs. For another, besides all that entertainment on the field, you might hold the winning ticket ($1) for a pizza, a bucket of night crawlers, or a few quarts of oil. Then there are those homemade pies at the concession stand, along with brats and all the rest. And after the game, the announcer invites the crowd to reconvene at Smiley's Pub or some such place.

While other slackers have been out curling, the Snow Hawks have been playing snowshoe baseball for many years and are virtually unbeatable. They used to have games in winter, with a blaze-orange ball, but the subzero weather and all that snow cut down on

★ ★

attendance. The hope is that someday it will be an Olympic demonstration sport. Wouldn't hurt the Lake Tomahawk economy one bit.

Games are played on Monday nights beginning late in June and ending in mid to late August (with an extra game on the Fourth of July, before the fireworks). The concession stand opens at 5:30 p.m., and the game starts at 7:30 p.m. Admission is free, but you'll have a chance to help out with expenses when the butterfly net comes around. Games are held at the athletic field in the center of town, a block west of Highway 47. Call (715) 277-2116 for details.

Shootout at Little Bo
Manitowish Waters

If John Dillinger thought things would cool off way up in Manitowish Waters (he is remembered in Racine, page 160, for his stopover there), he had another think coming. Well-dressed party of ten (John and his boys and their molls) checks into Little Bohemia Lodge. Hmmm. Isn't April a little early for fishing? Say, wasn't there a lot of excitement up in St. Paul . . . ? Somebody put two and two together and, lo and behold, on the night of April 22, 1934, the FBI showed up. Dogs barked, everybody came out shooting, and Dillinger and the guys got away, though three local men did not because the G-men mistook them for gang members and mowed 'em down. Three months later, on July 22, the Gs took Dillinger down for good outside the Biograph theater in Chicago.

Film director Michael Mann, being a stickler for historical accuracy, restaged the whole thing right here and on the seventy-fourth anniversary of the event when shooting scenes for *Public Enemies* (2009)— after restoring the lodge to 1930s condition, of course, and rearranging a few trees.

The entryway walls of Little Bohemia are papered with newspapers with headlines recalling all the excitement here: "Dillinger Gang Shoots Out of Trap," "Dillinger Abandons Car and Escapes." There's even a love letter from Johnnie to his girlfriend: "Darling: Gee! Honey I am

crazy to see you and when I see you again I am going to take you
with me if you care enough about me to want to go with me . . . lots
of love from Johnnie." The walls of the west wing of the lodge are
riddled with real bullet holes, and a display case shows what Johnnie
and the gang left behind in their hasty departure: the suitcase they carried the loot in, a can used for target practice, a suitcase neatly packed
with ties and shorts (white with blue stripes) and shirts, a can of Dr.
Lyons tooth powder, two tubes of Burma-Shave, a box of Ex-Lax. So,
Public Enemy Number One, or just another guy? You be the judge.

Today in its big dining rooms Little Bo (as the regulars having brandy
Manhattans at the bar call the place) serves walleye and ribeye to well-
behaved families on vacation. Located on Highway 51 south of Manitowish Waters. Open year-round, serving dinner nightly until 10:00
p.m., lunch in season. For more information call (715) 543-8800 or visit
www.littlebohemialodge.com.

Beep Beep *Beep*
Manitowoc

Manitowoc was still sleeping when a twenty-pound piece of metal
from outer space landed at the intersection of Park and North Eighth
Streets. Around dawn two policemen on patrol noticed it lying in the
street, mistook it for a piece of cardboard, and drove on. About an
hour later they came back to take a closer look, saw it was metal but
too hot to handle, and kicked it to the curb. It wasn't until noon, after
hearing the news that Sputnik IV had broken up in orbit, that they
hopped back in the car, returned to Park and Eighth, and boxed up the
hunk of metal, still warm.

After borrowing a Geiger counter from their friends at the firehouse
to be sure it wasn't radioactive, they made some phone calls and then
shipped it east. Tests at the Smithsonian and NASA confirmed that it
was the real thing, a fragment of Sputnik IV launched in the USSR on
May 14, 1960, Sputnik IV had encountered entry problems five days
later, wandered lonely as a cloud in outer space for the next two years,

★ ★

Rahr-West's souvenir of the space race.

and finally headed for Manitowoc on September 5, 1962. Some small charred fragments were later found on a church roof nearby; the rest of Sputnik IV probably ended up in Lake Michigan.

NASA created two replicas of the piece before returning the original to the Soviets (presumably after taking careful notes—this was at the height of the space race, after all), though some people in Manitowoc now regret not taking the Finders Keepers route. One replica is on

✦ ✦

display at the Rahr-West Art Museum—the thing had landed right outside its front door—and the other is at the Visitor Information Center.

A small, pink granite marker on the sidewalk (northwest corner) honors the recovery site, and a brass ring smack in the intersection marks the exact spot where the chunk landed. Manitowoc and the museum celebrate their place in space history, right in that intersection, with an annual Sputnikfest in September that includes the crowning of Miss Space Debris.

Rahr-West Art Museum, 610 North Eighth Street (corner of Park and North Eighth), is open 10:00 a.m. to 4:00 p.m. Monday through Friday ('til 8:00 p.m. Wednesday), 11:00 a.m. to 4:00 p.m. Saturday and Sunday. For more information call (920) 683-4501 or visit www .rahrwestartmuseum.org. or www.sputnikfest.com The Visitor Information Center is at Interstate 43 and Highway 151, exit 149.

Book Lovers
Markesan

Years ago the Dickmanns—Lloyd the farmer and Leonore the teacher—began collecting books. When the collection approached the million mark Lloyd converted his slurry tank, which once held tons of cow manure for fertilizer, to a bookstore. Now it is Castle Arkdale— crenellated trim, drawbridge, and all—the flagship of buildings around the farm that make up Happy Tales Books. The spiffiest slurry tank you ever saw—wood paneled and carpeted—holds many thousands of books, lovingly arranged mostly by subject but also for beauty, face up, the better to admire their covers. You'd think every book ever published must be here, somewhere, judging by the scope and such rarefied titles as *The History of the United States Told in One-Syllable Words* (1884), and they're all for sale.

Happy Tales Books is at W1778 County Highway K, along the south shore of Green Lake. There's no sign out front but you can see the castle from the road (it's the only one on K). Open 9:00 a.m. to 5:00 p.m.

A Spear and a Beer

Where can you spear a 200-million-year-old living fossil? At Lake Winnebago, in the heart of Wisconsin's Fox Valley. The prize? Hiawatha's Mishe-Nahma, the "King of Fishes," *Acipenser fulvescens,* aka the lake sturgeon. They're supposed to be pretty good eating once you pry off the bony plates and smoke 'em. And although the number of females allowed to be taken is strictly controlled, it is not impossible to fork some caviar on a very good day.

The catch is that, thanks to much-needed conservation limits, the sturgeon season is lightning short, so the window of opportunity closes quickly. You'll need a spear, some beer, a decoy, a chain saw with an ice bar (you may just want to pay the ten bucks and have a hole cut), a permit, and a shanty painted in Packer colors to park on the ice.

If you miss your great white, don't worry—sturgeons can live up to 150 years, which should give you more cracks at catching one than you're probably going to need. The upside is, should the Lord send a sturgeon to your hole, it'll be hard to miss, the record on Winnebago being 6 feet 7 inches and 188 pounds—though that may have been a spearer from last season who just surfaced.

The season opens the second Saturday in February and may close the third, so put down your $20 and take your chances—and don't neglect to be weighed, measured, sexed, and tagged by the waiting DNR biologist, especially if you get a fish. It's not easy—it took one guy from Fond du Lac twenty-three years of drinking Old Style to spear his first sturgeon; hence the saying, "Patience is a sturgeon." If you do get one, they'll hear about it in real time on Jerry Schneider's radio show over WMBE in Chilton.

Oshkosh or Fond du Lac is a good starting point for your sturgeon hunt to Lake Winnebago or one of the smaller lakes, such as Poygan.

Bill Casper of Fond du Lac at his fishing shack in fair weather. He spearheaded a movement to protect Lake Winnebago sturgeon by founding Sturgeon for Tomorrow.
ANDY KRAUSHAAR

★ ★

Saturday in summer months, other times by chance or appointment. 920-398-3375. No website. Nor do the Dickmanns advertise—they figure that people who are interested in books will find them.

Jurustic Park
Marshfield

Long ago, during the Iron Age, creatures inhabited the McMillan Marsh north of Marshfield. After many centuries they became extinct. Some succumbed to corrosion from acid rain; others were harvested for body

The mighty Marsh Dragon poses on the grounds of Jurustic Park.
CLYDE WYNIA

parts. Farmers used turtle shells for drinking cups, bird carcasses for shovels, and legs for bicycle forks . . .

Fortunately, enough body parts survived intact that most of the creatures could be reconstructed. We can see them today: the Whirlysaurus, the largest known airborne marsh creature; the Bong Bird, whose wing feathers supply the Fiskars plant in Spencer with blades for grass clippers; the Marsh King, which dressed in drag and ruled the marsh; the Positron, whose head bobs in agreement; the Marsh Mouse, which leveled enemies with methane gas; the Feathered Turtle, slow to get off the ground but once up, up there for months; Dorks.

These huge and complex rusted-metal creatures and their history spring from the wide-ranging imagination of Clyde Wynia, a retired attorney. Where does he get his ideas? "I just keep digging in the marsh." How long does it take to make one? He says he doesn't know and doesn't care. "All I want to do is play."

To get there, turn left off Highway 97 as it leaves Marshfield onto Highway E. Go about 3.5 miles north on E, then west on U-shaped Sugar Bush Lane for 0.5 mile. More marsh creatures and malarkey at www.jurustic.com.

You're Not in Neenah Anymore
Menasha

The Tayco Street Bridge Museum is small for a museum. Picture your 9-by-12 rug with two corners lopped off and that gives you an idea of the floor space here (it's sort of hexagonal). But it has two levels, connected by a metal spiral stairway; exhibits that tell much of the history of the Tayco Street Bridge, the Fox River channel that flows under it, and the city of Menasha; and three upholstered benches where you can ponder the meaning of it all.

You will learn that Jean Nicolet probably stopped here after his grand entrance in Green Bay in 1634, holding councils with Indian tribes as he continued along the Fox. (Whether he was still wearing his Chinese coat—he'd been looking for passage to the East—is not noted.)

★ ★

And, oh, for the days when steamboats hauled logs to the tub-and-pail factory on weekdays and offered pleasure cruises on weekends. Today, except for an occasional barge, most of the traffic is your small-scale variety, headed for Lake Winnebago for a day of sailing or fishing, from the Appleton Yacht Club or Little Lake Butte des Morts.

You will learn about bridges that have been built and rebuilt on this site since 1859, such as the wooden drawbridge that collapsed in 1886 as a large herd of cattle was crossing, and the bridge dedicated in 1929, when airplanes dropped flowers, the mayor's daughter cut the ribbon at midnight, and Menashans—defying another cattlelike mishap—danced the night away on the new bridge. A segment of that bridge collapsed in 1989, but three of its four stone towers—one at each corner—remain (well, one's a replica). One houses the little museum and another the bridge-tending operation, which is now computerized and even remote controlled from the Racine Street bridge to the east. Too bad—the human bridge tender must have had lots of fun at the control panel, with its buttons plainspokenly labeled KLAXONS, CLOSE, NEARLY CLOSED, NEARLY OPEN, FULLY OPEN, SIRENS.

Today's Tayco Street Bridge has four lanes, two sidewalks, powder blue beams, and one leaf. If you suddenly hear *clangclangclangclangclang!* while you're in the museum, head for the door. That means the bridge is about to open, and state law says you must scurry outside and stand behind the gate until the bridge closes again.

Incidentally, unlike most of the world's rivers (but like the Nile in Egypt, for one), the Fox River flows north—the Lower Fox, that is, which flows from the north end of Lake Winnebago toward lower Green Bay (the bay). The Upper Fox, which is in the lower part of the state, flows southward. Geography works in mysterious ways.

The Tayco Street Museum is open from 10:00 a.m. to 7:00 p.m. daily during navigation season, May through October. From Highway 41, follow Commercial Street (Highway 114) through Neenah to the bridge, where Menasha begins. For more information call 920-967-5155.

Death's Door

It's hard to believe that Wisconsin's Nantucket, beautiful Door County, gets its name from Porte des Morts—"Death's Door," the treacherous passage between Green Bay and Lake Michigan that has claimed thousands of vessels and hundreds of lives over the years. The most famous of these wrecks may have been the explorer La Salle's hide-laden schooner the *Griffin*, which disappeared in high seas in 1680.

The legend of a seemingly impassable strait goes back at least to the ongoing wars between the Winnebago and Potawatomi tribes, which stretched across the passage between the northern tip of the peninsula and Washington Island. A fire beacon set by the Winnebagoes to lead a Potawatomi war party toward the rocky shoals caused a flotilla of canoes to be dashed against the rocks. Hundreds of warriors were killed, and their bodies continued to wash up on nearby Detroit Island for years. In 1871 a hundred vessels were reported lost in "The Door." And in 1913, during the "great blow" when hurricane-force gales lashed the Great Lakes for three November days, twenty ships with 248 men went down. Today, even with sophisticated navigational aids and charts, only the most experienced of sailors attempt the Porte des Morts.

The Door County Maritime Museum in Gills Rock, at 12724 Wisconsin Bay Road, is a good place to learn more about the history of the Door. And if you would like to sail, boat, or arrange for a charter, the chamber of commerce Web site (www.doorcountyvacations.com) can point you in the right direction.

The Parade of Beef is the creative portion of the annual Beef-A-Rama festival in Minocqua. Local businesspeople cook roasts on their storefront sidewalks, dream up a theme, and then parade the roasts down the main street. Here the Northwoods Wildlife Center, a hospital for injured and orphaned wild animals, tries to revive its entry. The parade ends at Torpy Park, where the roasts are sliced and served up in hundreds of beef sandwiches. Beef-A-Rama takes place on the last Saturday in September.

Some, Seeing a Hole, Leave It at That

Montello

Mother Nature gave Montello lakes, rivers, and babbling brooks. Irving Daggett gave Montello four waterfalls, one of them 40 feet high, right in the center of town. The waterfall site was once a working granite quarry, Montello's leading industry for almost a century. The end of quarrying in 1976 left Montello with an enormous hole in the ground, but Daggett, a local real estate agent and Christmas tree farmer, saw possibilities there.

Where once the ground shook at blasting time, a little musical church plays recorded hymns, and swans glide across the old granite quarry at Montello. ERICA SCHLUETER

★ ★

Trivia

Granite from the quarry at Montello won a gold medal at the 1893 World's Fair as "100% harder than any other granite." Purplish red in color, it was chosen from more than 280 other granite samples in 1897 as the monument stone for Ulysses S. Grant's tomb.

He bought the big hole and paid for the construction of the four falls that tumble year-round into the quarry, which now is filled with spring water to depths of 100 feet. He also added a miniature church that rings with religious or patriotic carillon music at various times through-out the day and, in a quarry alcove at Christmastime, a life-size nativity scene. The quarry property occupies about ten acres along Montello Street (Highway 23) between Daggett Realty and Kwik Trip, and incor-porates a fifth waterfall, which the Lions Club built back in 1969.

Two other imposing sights lie just west of downtown on Highway 23 near the Marquette County Courthouse. One is the largest tree in Wisconsin, a giant cottonwood. The last time it was measured, in 1978, it was 138 feet high and 23 feet around. The other is Le Maison Granit, an awesome, plum-colored mansion built in 1909 of, yes, Mon-tello granite!

In Madison We Call Them Personhole Covers

Neenah

No matter how far Badgers may roam, home won't seem quite so far away if they remember to pause at the curb or crosswalk. There they can likely gaze down upon the words NEENAH FOUNDRY CO. NEENAH, WIS.

Most drainage grates and manhole covers bear those words because Neenah Foundry has been meeting the storm-water-management needs

Kissinger: More Than a Lady-Killer

It was Henry Kissinger's lucky day when Meldon Maguire came along. Meldon has a dairy farm near Mosinee and serves on the board of supervisors.

Late one night in September 1997, along Highway 153 about 9 miles west of Mosinee, Meldon was heading home from a supervisors' meeting and saw flashing taillights up ahead. He stopped his truck at the scene and put on his red "First Responders" vest. (First Responders respond to emergencies and offer assistance.)

Meldon got out and saw guys in suits standing around a big limousine with the windshield all bashed in. The limo had hit a deer. Everybody was okay, and the suits asked Meldon for a ride to their hotel. Meldon cleared out the wrappers and pop cans ("Hey, I got three kids"), every-one piled into the truck, and off they went.

Someone said, "This is Dr. Henry Kissinger," but the name didn't ring a bell. "I knew he had something to do with Nixon," said Meldon, "but I was only about five at that time. I almost asked him what he did for a living. Thank God I didn't."

The next day Meldon received a special invitation to join Kissinger and his entourage, as well as former president Gerald Ford, at the renowned Marshfield Clinic, where an addition was being dedicated to another local boy, Melvin Laird, U.S. secretary of defense in the Nixon cabinet (1969–73).

It was a very full week for Meldon Maguire. He and his wife, Karen, had had a new baby just four days earlier and named her Fawne—before the Kissinger limo–deer accident.

of the world for the past century—not only manhole covers and drainage gates but also catch-basin covers; gutter inlets; bridge, subway, and building drains; trench covers; valves and gates; and tree grates. If it's man-made and drains into the earth, Neenah Foundry is there.

The company began making plowshares in 1872 and later expanded the product line to include barn-door rollers, sleigh shoes, bean pots, and other cast-iron items. It cast its first manhole covers and sewer grates in 1904. If you're lucky enough, you can even get a souvenir manhole cover with your name on it, like the one that today graces the hearth of Casa Feldman.

Even as you sleep Neenah Foundry is serving you. ERICA SCHLUETER

A well-coifed mannequin models a straitjacket, a relic of the Northern State Hospital for the Insane, now Winnebago Mental Health Institute.

Nurse Ratched, You're Fired!

Oshkosh

Northern State Hospital for the Insane admitted its first patient on April 21, 1873. Many improvements have been made since that day, including a change of name to Winnebago Mental Health Institute (WMHI). Today this modern psychiatric facility treats about 300 children and adults of all ages in its specialized programs.

A museum on the grounds tells about past practices, patients, and personnel. On the first floor, exhibits display each of the twenty-six spoons that one patient swallowed, as well as an impressive variety of items consumed by others—buttons, leather straps, a bedspring, scissors, checkers, a rubber heel, a fingernail file, a toothbrush handle, a thermometer, a crochet hook, tacks, wire, pieces of slate, and coal. A color photograph that apparently was taken during surgery shows where several dollars' worth of change ended up. Another exhibit indicates the ingenuity of restless patients in making "keys for elopement"—escape, that is—and weapons.

Upstairs are five more rooms of exhibits. They include uniforms that staff members formerly wore (today they usually wear street clothes), an electroshock-therapy machine, medical instruments in cabinets, mannequins in treatment, a wicker body basket, and laboratory equipment. Photographs and an audiocassette offer further details from the past, such as statistics on lobotomies. The entire presentation helps visitors appreciate the progress that has been made over the past century in treating troubled individuals along the shores of Asylum Bay on Lake Winnebago.

The Julaine Farrow Museum, at 4150 Sherman, is housed in what formerly was the superintendent's residence; it includes many original furnishings. The museum is located in the northwest part of the 250-acre grounds that WMHI shares with the Wisconsin Resource Center (for about 400 corrections inmates with mental health problems) and the Drug Abuse Center (population about 200). It is located a few miles north of Oshkosh.

From exit 120 eastbound (Highway 110/Algoma Boulevard) of Highway 41, immediately take the first left turn (Snell Road) and follow Snell for about 4 miles. It leads directly to the grounds. The museum is open from 1:00 to 3:30 p.m. on Thursday only, February through October. For more information call (920) 235-4910.

Mourning Becomes DuWayne

I don't know about you, but there are mornings when I wake up and would like nothing more than to blast a bird of peace, particularly if one's been cooing outside my window since six. Well, in September 2003, after a two-year court battle, Wisconsin's first-ever dove season opened. It all had begun when 22,000 of the 27,000 or so people who turned out for a Natural Resources Board meeting (which usually draws as many as 37) voted to shoot the official state bird of peace.

DuWayne Johnsrud, a state legislator from Eastman, led the charge against the admittedly not very hard to take dove (whose mourning, after all, does have a *u* in it). He even went so far as to fricassee a mess of them in his capitol office (don't know where he got them, but there were noticeably fewer pigeons on the porticos that week) and offer tiny little drumsticks to all takers to make his point. Taste-wise, they are said to run somewhat to the crow side of squab, but as the French say, the sauce is everything. Johnsrud noted, "There are those people out there who don't want you to eat anything that's got a face on it."

Now, the season runs from September through October, with a limit of fifteen things with faces on them per day. It offers a special challenge to hunters because mourning doves fly erratically, even when they're not being fired upon. The cleverest mourning doves spend most of those two months perched on power lines after word spread that a utility company had warned hunters that all kinds of problems could result from shooting at birds on power lines. Each bird that does not survive the season rewards the hunter with about half an ounce of mourning dove.

The downside is that at one time, Wisconsin had the largest nestings of the now-extinct passenger pigeon, 850 square miles at one sitting—an

Continued on page 80

estimated 136 million birds. (A historic marker at the exit 46 rest stop of westbound Interstate 94 south of Black River Falls describes the scene.) The last was shot by a conservationist in 1899, making the woods safe, once again, for acorns.

If this sort of thing interests you, you can contact the Department of Natural Resources regarding mourning doves, as well as other things with faces that you can hunt in Wisconsin. Call (608) 266-2621 or visit www.dnr.state.wi.us. The Web site even offers recipes, such as Doves in Mushroom Soup, which calls for two cans of cream of mushroom soup and thirty tiny dove breasts.

Leapin' Lizards
Oshkosh

If you didn't find just the right statuary for the garden at FAST in Sparta (see page 216), you might browse the grounds of Schettl's near Oshkosh. The main business of Schettl's Freight Sales is hardware and building supplies, but its line of "so-tacky-it's-way-beyond-cool stuff," as one admirer puts it, is the big attraction here. Gigantic insects, roosters, circus animals, sharks, sundaes, and cowboy boots—they cover the ground, they perch on rooftops, they bound through the air. Elephants look striking against the backdrop of barn, silo, and cornfields across the road.

How many dinosaurs do you know that have black leather seats? The one at Schettl's does. Just climb a flight of stairs to mouth level, step right in, and settle down, the better to admire the rest of the decor, which carries out a prehistoric theme—the little nest of baby dinosaurs, the dragon collection on the windowsill.

This would also be the place to shop for Cinderella's coach. Schettl's has several and shows them bearing such passengers as a mountain goat, an Egyptian mummy, and a blonde vamp in a red, white, and blue miniskirt. Other outsize display cases resemble glass gazebos and are occupied by British royalty, Laurel and Hardy, Marilyn Monroe, and Elvis. Display is definitely Mel Schettl's forte.

After you remember what you came to Shettl's for—a bathtub? siding? batteries?—you can consider taking home something special that may have caught your eye. A life-size set of Blues Brothers, the moose that ate Oshkosh, the Statue of Liberty . . . The vast collection is available for rent, and some of it is for sale.

Schettl's is at 5105 County Road S. Hours are 8:00 a.m. to 6:00 p.m. during the week, 8:00 a.m. to 5:00 p.m. Saturday, and 11:00 a.m. to 4:00 p.m. Sunday. Call (920) 426-1681 or see www.mschettl.com.

A safari at Schettl's ends badly when a rhino tips over a Suzuki with Texas plates and a headless driver. ERICA SCHLUETER

You Went a Long Way, Baby Doe

Her eyes were blue—bluer than Lake Winnebago—her ankles were strong, and her hemline revealed more of her lower extremities (it wasn't nice to say "legs") than the Oshkosh of 1877 was accustomed to seeing. The only female entrant in the figure-skating contest, Elizabeth Bonduel McCourt won first place, a box of chocolates, and the heart of a handsome spectator, Harvey Doe.

The couple married and moved to the mining town of Central City, Colorado, where Harvey proceeded to run his share of the Doe family fortune into a shoestring. The mine shut down, and so did the marriage ("You have of corse herd of my sad sad loss in loosing my darling Babe I am heart broken about it I shal go crazey," sniveled Harvey in a letter home to the folks in Oshkosh). But new possibilities opened up for Elizabeth, or "Baby." (She acquired the nickname in the rowdy mining towns, as in "There goes a beautiful —.")

In time Baby's picture was appearing on saloon beer trays and calendars, and at Leadville she met Horace Tabor, whose silver mines had made him one of the wealthiest men in the West and, by appointment, a United States senator. His plain and plucky wife, Augusta, could not compete.

In 1883 Horace and Baby celebrated their wedding at the Willard Hotel in Washington, D.C. (Baby stopped off in Oshkosh to model her silks and furs for the town gossips.)

President Chester Arthur, distinguished guests, and a contingent from Oshkosh attended. Baby's gift from Horace was a $75,000 necklace of jewels that Queen Isabella had hocked so that Columbus could discover America. Later they had two daughters, Elizabeth Bonduel Lillie Tabor and Rosemary Echo Silver Dollar Honeymoon Tabor ("Silver Dollar" for short).

Does Oshkosh have a statue, a plaza, or even a bench at the skating rink in memory of the "Silver Queen," the most fabulous woman to emerge from its pioneer era—this Marla Maples, this Monica of the Middle West? It does not, and the Colorado Historical Society has all of Baby Doe's memorabilia, leaving not so much as a marabou feather from her $7,000 wedding gown for the folks back in Wisconsin. But in 1972 the University of Wisconsin–Oshkosh produced *The Ballad of Baby Doe,* the 1956 opera by Douglas Moore that had its New York City Opera premiere in 1958 and is now recognized as the quintessential American opera. It's got politics! the Wild West!! the American dream!!!

The Ballad of Baby Doe tells the whole story, right down to the day in 1935 that Baby Doe was found dead—frozen with two weeks' stiffness into the shape of a cross—in a shack outside Horace's Matchless Mine. Horace had gone bankrupt years earlier when the country abandoned the silver standard. "Hang on to the Matchless. It will make millions again," were his dying words in 1899. And that is what Baby Doe did, though it meant shuffling around town with gunnysacks on her feet for shoes in her last years, and finally dying in rags.

★ ★

A Man. A Plan.
Poniatowski

About 5,000 people from all over the world have driven a maze of county roads in search of a certain 1885 white frame building with a Blatz sign out front.

It was Gesicki's Bar, the home of the 45 x 90 Club, and behind the bar was the membership book that everyone came to sign. It attested that they had stood in the exact center of the northern half of the western hemisphere—45 degrees north latitude and 90 degrees west longitude, or halfway between the North Pole and the equator, and halfway between the Greenwich meridian and the international date line. Of the other three spots like it on the globe, two are underwater and the third is in the middle of China.

John Gesicki instigated the official recognition and landmark. He had a little park outside of town all ready when the U.S. Geological Survey came to plant the marker in 1969. He started the club, and after John died, his widow, Loretta, offered the book and the pen. But the membership book is closed now. In 2003 Loretta decided she needed a rest, so she sold the bar, packed up the book, and moved to an apartment in Wausau. What once was Gesicki's Bar is now a private residence.

When Poniatowski pilgrims came through the door, Loretta used to play a recording of Peter and Lou Berryman singing this song:

Exactly half the way from the Equator to the Pole
A quarter of the way around the planet as a whole
It's very hard to find it on a map o' county roads
Ridiculously easy on a four-inch globe
Magellan's men said Captain have we gotten very far
We're writing to our mothers just to tell 'em where we are
The Captain said our longitude is fifty on the dot
I don't know where we are but I can tell you where we're not.
A quarter of the way from top to bottom of our earth

A quarter of the way around the planet of our birth
Speaking cartographically it's not extreme to say
It's the most important 'towski in the USA.
What is on the tip of every schoolkid's tongue
What I mean of course besides a wad of gum
The name of a location every grownup knows
Of a church, a couple taverns, and a school that's closed.
I asked an old cartographer where he would rather be
He mumbled there's a place that's always fascinated me
I'll prob'ly mispronounce it he admitted with a sigh
It's P-O-N-I-A-T-O "duBULLYU" s-k-i.
Poniatowski . . .

Poniatowski is located about 12 miles west of Wausau and does not appear on all maps. From Highway 29 west of Wausau, go north on Highway H, then west on Highway U to Poniatowski. Follow the signs to the spot that marks the center of the northern half of the Western Hemisphere.

Roadside Religion
Princeton

Ken Soda has always been an original thinker. In the 1950s, for instance, when he and all the neighboring farmers were raising the same crops and stock, Ken took the long view and switched to mint, of all things. "You have to do something harder and more specialized to make a go of this business" was his thinking. Wise move, as it turned out, and just the beginning of a lifetime of innovation that led to his latest creation, a bowling ball rosary.

A few years ago Ken was browsing among the bowling balls at St. Vinnie's thrift store and took home a few that caught his eye, and later a few more, and more, until about 150 of them lined his driveway. But the bowling balls had far more potential, thought Ken. Brainstorming with friends provided the breakthrough idea of a rosary, and Ken got busy.

It's a few yards past the bowling ball bush.

Mint farming had given Ken plenty of experience in improvisation—he had had to invent his own mint-farming equipment. And recently he'd created a 64-foot medicine wheel on his property. So a rosary was simply a matter of some stainless steel cable, plastic things for spacers, and a loader tractor with a boom to hoist it into place. A stainless steel hubcap from a passing car on Highway J became the center piece. Ken was pleased. It was both religious and sports-minded.

Today most of the mint farming is done by the two sons of Ken and Eunice Soda. (Eunice collects statues of the Blessed Mother, about 1,200 so far, no two alike.) They represent the fifth generation on this land, going back to Ken's great-grandfather, who latched onto President Lincoln's Homestead Act in 1862. At a time when many young people are fleeing the family farm, Ken's sons have no interest in living anywhere else. And chances for a sixth generation here are good, with several young grandchildren on the scene. Landscape historian John Warfield Simpson writes about the Soda family and farm with awe and admiration in *Yearning for the Land*.

The bowling ball rosary is even a destination on Geocache, the outdoor treasure-hunt game in which people zoom around the countryside using Global Positioning Systems to locate cache sites with special names, in this case "Great Balls." Anyone else can simply drive west on Highway J from Princeton for about 5 miles and, just past the Green Lake–Marquette County line, watch for the bowling ball bush at the end of the Sodas' driveway (Ken made it from an antique hay rake). Slow down and you'll soon see the rosary.

Odd Bedfellows
Ripon

Ripon has the distinction of being the birthplace of both the Republican Party and the Wisconsin Phalanx, a distinctly Badger take on communism in which stock was sold, real estate purchased, and communal adherents rewarded according to their usefulness.

★ ★

The socialist band was organized in Kenosha and led in the spring of 1844 to the Ceresco Valley (named for Ceres, the goddess of grain) near Ripon by Warren Chase, a follower of the French philosopher and socialist Charles Fourier. The group planted grain and built a gristmill, carpenter shop, school, and the longhouse (which still stands today). Although it was ideal, it was not free. Board was 63 cents a week (on the other hand, wages averaged out to 7½ cents an hour, and the cost of feeding and clothing the entire extended family was deducted). And while it promoted equality, some were more equal than others in their skills—which, in time, caused some resentment by the less useful.

Still, utopia does not mean "nowhere" for nothing. Ceresco was a success until a life without "rum, vulgarity, and profanity" seemed to wear on some, particularly after free-love devotees moved in. Others, tired of communal life, set up their own households. But at its height, 200 communists lived in rural Ripon, some of whom, idealists still, stayed on after the community was sold off in 1850 to join in the formation of the Republican Party, the flower of the strong Wisconsin antislavery movement.

The one-room schoolhouse where this meeting took place on March 20, 1854, is now a historic site at 303 Blackburn Street, about a block off Ripon's main street. Hours are 10:00 a.m. to 4:00 p.m. daily from Memorial Day to Labor Day, weekends in September and October. The longhouse is at 26–34 Warren Street.

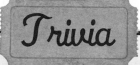

Trivia

Bemis Manufacturing Company of Sheboygan Falls is the world's largest manufacturer of toilet seats.

Praise the Lord and Pass the Mortar

Rudolph

The Grotto Gardens and Wonder Cave represent the lifelong labors of parish priest Phillip J. Wagner. This site is all the more remarkable if you know that Wagner started here with a potato field and no mortaring experience. His first attempt at grotto building, in 1928, consisted of stacking up rocks. When he realized he'd also need mortar, he stirred it in a bread pan with a kitchen spoon. He got the hang of it, though, and over the next thirty years, Wagner and an equally dedicated member of the parish transformed the potato field into an extraordinary collection of shrines and grottoes.

The Wonder Cave makes this religious grotto unique among others in Wisconsin. From the outside the Wonder Cave looks like a hill of rocks among trees and plantings. Inside, however, it has not only cave ambience—a passageway that winds up and down and around, water trickling down the walls—but also organ music, statuary, and biblical reminders in the form of little tin sheets with perforated words and images, backlighted with colored bulbs. The cave is entirely aboveground (unusual for a cave), and the man-made passageway is a fifth of a mile long.

The Grotto Gardens and Wonder Cave are located on the grounds of St. Philip's Parish, 6957 Grotto Avenue, Rudolph. The Wonder Cave and a gift shop are open daily 10:00 a.m. to 5:00 p.m. Memorial Day through Labor Day. The Grotto Gardens are open year-round, no charge; there's a small admission fee for the Wonder Cave. For more information call (715) 435-3120.

The Woods Are Alive with the Sound of Motor Toboggans

Sayner

Eighty years ago Carl Eliason rigged up the world's first snowmobile by combining an outboard motor, part of a Ford Model T radiator, two bicycle chains, and two pairs of downhill skis. He painted the seat red and called the whole thing a "motor toboggan." In the garage behind

★ ★

Eliason's Grocery, he kept on fiddling with the design and built forty more motor toboggans, almost no two alike.

For quite a few years Eliason Snowmobile Manufacture had the field to itself, but then along came the competition and their copywriters, with names such as Arctic Cat, Ski-Doo, Sno-Traveler, and the Ice Cycle (a 1964 creation that was supposed to be portable but turned out to be too heavy to lug from the family station wagon to the ice). These share a room but not center stage with Eliason's motor toboggan at the Vilas County Historical Museum. Some rare outboard motors are here, too, as well as a hand-powered motor made of wood, carved propeller and all.

But the museum has much, much more. Beyond the armies of old dolls and passels of sewing machines and typewriters and kitchen equipment is a room of surprises in taxidermy: wildebeest, Cape buffalo, warthog, eland—all strangers to this neck of the woods. They're the trophies of a Sayner man who had had his fill of white-tailed deer and went after big game in Africa.

Look for the lumberjack with the big blue ox outside 217 Main Street (Highway 155) in Sayner, just 1 block north of Highway N. Open 10:00 a.m. to 4:00 p.m. daily from Memorial Day to mid-October. Call (715) 542-3388 for more information, or visit www .northern-wisconsin.com/museum.

Elegy for a Spatula
Seymour

Charlie Nagreen of Hortonville was only fifteen years old in 1885 when he arrived in Seymour by ox-drawn wagon to set up his meatball stand at the Outagamie County Fair. When meatballs turned out to be a less-than-ideal finger food (especially since he cooked them in butter), Charlie smooshed a meatball between two slices of bread and called it a hamburger.

For the next sixty-five years, Hamburger Charlie was a fixture at the fair. In 1989 Seymour underlined its place in culinary history by cooking

The grill that cooked the world's biggest hamburger. They didn't try to flip it. ERICA SCHLUETER

and serving to 13,000 people a 5,520-pound hamburger—the world's largest, as recorded in the *Guinness Book of World Records*. When you come to think of it, it's amazing they had to go that high to get the record.

In 1999 word arrived from Montana of a 6,040-pound hamburger. Home of the Hamburger, Inc., graciously hung back until 2001 to let the Montanans bask in glory, and then cooked an 8,266-pound burger (about fifty-three cows' worth) to reclaim the title.

The Hamburger Hall of Fame museum on Main Street, which documented Seymour's place in hamburger history, is no longer open, but the annual Burger Fest, with parade, bun run, bun toss, and ketchup slide, remains an annual event, the first Saturday in August. Details at www.homeofthehamburger.org.

A cure for cabin fever in 1939, smelt wrestling at the
Smelt Carnival in Marinette. WISCONSIN HISTORICAL SOCIETY

From Plumbing, Art
Sheboygan

Visitors tend to linger in the washrooms at the John Michael Kohler
Arts Center. There's a lot to see.

One of the men's rooms tells the social history of architecture in
vivid hand-painted tiles, with such phrases posted over the fixtures as
"Celebrating Another Conquest," "Boldness Has Genius," "Aspiring
Toward Heaven," and "Defending the Castle." In a colorful women's
room, hand-painted tiles and fixtures depict jewelry and sunglasses
strewn across the countertop, a thong soaking in the sink, a dress
hanging on the wall, and imagery of women—from Medusa to a Play-
boy Bunny.

The six artist-decorated washrooms are the epitome of the unique Arts/Industry residency program funded by Kohler Co., which encourages artists to explore materials and equipment at its nearby plumbing-ware factory. The collaboration has produced many more works, some of which appear in one of the galleries. They include a large coffee cup that flushes, Ken and Barbie andirons, and a Squeaky Fromme nightlight.

This water-pistol bouquet in delft style, with hand-painted and hand-glazed tiles, appears over a urinal at the Arts Center. The artist was Ann Agee. COURTESY JOHN MICHAEL KOHLER ARTS CENTER

Another gallery exhibits works of self-taught Midwestern artists. Among them have been the elaborate chicken-and-turkey-bone towers of the prolific artist Eugene Von Bruenchenhein, a Milwaukee baker who so adored his wife, Marie, that he fashioned elegant crowns of ordinary materials for her. Another time the center invited Sheboyga- nians to create art measuring no more than 1-inch-by-1-inch-by-1-inch and displayed their 1,700 pieces—tiny paintings and sculptures and furniture—along measuring tapes.

There are surprises elsewhere, too, such as the life-size ceramic horse by Deborah Butterfield in the formal dining room of the Kohler family mansion, which stands at the corner of the recently expanded Arts Center.

The John Michael Kohler Arts Center, 608 New York Avenue, opens at 10:00 a.m. daily, year-round. (Be there when the doors open and you probably can safely tour all six washrooms. At other times try a stakeout, followed by a knock on the door.) It closes at 5:00 p.m. Monday, Wednesday, and Friday; at 8:00 p.m. Tuesday and Thursday; and at 4:00 p.m. Saturday and Sunday.

To get there, take exit I-43 (exit 126) onto Highway 23 East, which becomes Kohler Memorial Drive and then Erie Avenue. Continue east to Sixth Street, turn right, and follow Sixth Street 4 blocks south to New York Avenue. The entrance to the Arts Center is on New York Avenue between Sixth and Seventh Streets. For more information about one of the most unusual arts organizations in the United States, call (920) 458-6144 or visit www.jmkac.org.

Sheboygan Says "Aloha!"
Sheboygan

From bratwurst to surfing, Sheboygan constantly surprises. The annual Dairyland Surf Classic held at Northside Beach is the largest freshwater surfing competition in the world, and its champion is Larry Williams, who surfs here almost year-round.

The water is pretty cold in August—what must January be like?

Mostly frozen, says Larry (aka Longboard), who leashes his ankle to his board so it doesn't get away "because it's quite a challenge to retrieve a board that's trapped under an iceberg." An iceberg? Yes, icebergs, snow squalls, legendary gales, and waves greater than 24 feet several times a year. Having surfed here for more than forty years, he knows his Lake Michigan.

Mercifully, the Dairyland Classic takes place in summer, over Labor Day weekend, and it attracts surfers to the Malibu of the Midwest from as far away as Hawaii, Australia, and New Zealand. You can see Larry and his twin brother, Lee (aka the Water Flea), in *Step into Liquid* (a kind of *Endless Summer, Part 3*), which was filmed here and elsewhere in 2000 and won Best Documentary at the Maui Film Festival.

An Indian chief peers out at passers-by at James Tellen's Woodland Sculpture Garden. Created in the 1940s and '50s, Tellen's cement sculptures—gnomes, castles, Saint Peter, Lincoln—follow a plank pathway into the woods. The site is on Evergreen Drive, a block from Lake Michigan in the Black River Point area south of Sheboygan. To arrange a tour, call the John Michael Kohler Arts Center, (920) 458-6144.

Divers report greatly improved visibility when a shipwreck, like the *Lottie Cooper* in Sheboygan, is on land.

The Wreck of the *Lottie Cooper*

Sheboygan

The *Lottie Cooper* was a three-masted schooner that foundered in a howling northeast gale on the night of April 9, 1894. It went down in the Sheboygan harbor and lay there for the next century. Recently her remains were discovered on the harbor floor, during surveying work for construction of a marina. The remains were recovered from the murky floor, reassembled in their original positions, and are now on display on the grounds of the marina.

An estimated 10,000 ships have been lost on the Great Lakes—700 in Lake Michigan, 60 off Sheboygan, and about a dozen right in the harbor. (Some were hauled up, pumped out, and put back in service, only to sink two or three more times.) *Lottie* represents them all because she's the only recovered shipwreck on display on the Great Lakes today. Text and drawings tell more about her saga.

There are self-tours here as well as guided tours for groups. Call (920) 458-2974 for information.

The Pole of Babel
Sheboygan

Driving by on I-43, you might think that the gargantuan American flag flapping in the distance must be the biggest one in the whole wide world. It is not, but the thing that holds it up is the tallest flagpole.

The pole is 338 feet high, weighs 65 tons, and is planted in a 550-ton block of concrete that's 40 feet deep. It's 6 feet wide at the base and has a ladder inside for the person who has to change the light-bulb in the beacon. It marks the headquarters of the Acuity insurance company.

What brought all this on? A mere 40 mph wind, which took down Acuity's previous flagpole, which was pretty high, but the new one is twice as high. And the flag? It's 120 feet by 60 feet and weighs 300 pounds. Each star is 3 feet high and each stripe is 4½ feet wide.

You'd think that would make it the tallest flagpole not only in the nation, but in the world, the galaxy, the cosmos! But no, there's a taller one, by about 90 feet—the *tallest*—and it's in the Middle East, not the Middle West. Visible from four countries bordering the Gulf of Aqaba on the Red Sea, it's in Aqaba, Jordan, but it's not the flag of Jordan. It's a royal flag, of the Hashemite dynasty, which reigns in Amman today but originated somewhere else. Or something like that. It's complicated.

America's tallest flagpole is on the south side of Sheboygan. For a closer look, take exit 123 off I-43.

And the world's largest flag is a flag of Israel. It's 2,165 feet long and 330 feet wide and weighs 5.7 tons. When it was revealed in late 2007, its producer, a Filipino evangelical Christian, explained that she'd

★ ★

been asked to undertake the project by the Lord, who apparently did not say anything about a flagpole. The flag lies on the desert sands at the Masada airfield near the Dead Sea, with large stones anchoring it down.

When Life Gives You Cabbage
Shiocton

"The wife and I needed a fund-raiser for the church," says Wayne "Ace" Van Stratten. "The chicken dinner was getting old. I saw pumpkin chucking on TV, and said, 'We could throw pumpkins,' and my wife said, 'Why don't we throw cabbages? We've got thousands of tons of them.'"

She's not exaggerating. Every year the Great Lakes Kraut factory in nearby Bear Creek mines about 170,000 tons of raw cabbage from local fields and processes them into 50,000 tons of sauerkraut. Needless to say, Great Lakes leads the world in sauerkraut.

So cabbage it was. Ace spent hours researching what kinds of machines were best for chucking cabbages and came up with interesting possibilities, such as catapults and trebuchets, like the ones the ancient Romans built to hurl boulders at invaders. That kind of thing turned out to come in handy, along with a 72-foot air cannon that can send a cabbage about 1,500 feet downrange. "We definitely close the airport for the day," says Ace. "Don't want any low-flying planes involved." While pumpkins are okay and acorn squash is good too, cabbage is more fun, he says, because it leaves a nice vapor trail of leaves across the sky.

Meanwhile, at the Little Sprouts Competition, kids are firing brussels sprouts from little table-top trebuchets and catapults they built themselves. A recent winner threw a sprout 57 feet. Later in the day, as the last cabbage leaf is drifting to earth, it's time for another exciting event: cabbage wrestling. Contestants compete in a 12-foot pond of sauerkraut and ice-cold water in two-minute refereed matches. Anything goes. Takedown wins.

Green Bay Packers tickets and other great prizes reward the winners throughout the day. The Shiocton World Championship Cabbage Chuck and Sauerkraut Wrestling Festival takes place in Shiocton Lake Park in September. For more information visit www.sauerkraut wrestling.com.

Al Johnson's goats. WISCONSIN DEPARTMENT OF TOURISM (GARY KNOWLES)

And Swedish Meatballs under the Roof

Sister Bay

Regardless of whether or not Scandinavian houses still have sod roofs, Al Johnson thought a sod roof would be a nice touch for the Swedish restaurant he opened in 1948. The eatery was housed in a log building that was shipped in pieces from Norway to Sister Bay. A friend donated a goat named Oscar to complete the picture, and after that Al didn't

★ ★

have to worry about advertising. The word spread, crowds gathered, and they still do.

It's best to arrive in some conventional manner, such as by car or on foot. When curious people from Marinette landed their helicopter on

They Couldn't Eat Just One

In the 1860s a woodcutter named John A. "Long John" Johnson was well known around Sister Bay for his huge appetite. In *Exploring Door County,* Craig Charles writes that a local storekeeper bet Long John five dollars that he couldn't eat five dozen eggs in one sitting. A quixotic bet to be sure, but the big guy took it "on the condition the prize included a pint of whiskey. Long John is said to have eaten all the eggs, drunk the whiskey and gone home to top it off with a loaf of bread and a pail of mllk."

More than a century later, Wisconsin men are carrying on this proud tradition. One possible reincarnation of Long John is Dennis Leffin of Kohler, who as a growing boy in the 1950s won not only more bratwurst-eating contests than anyone in the history of Sheboygan County, but also eating contests in watermelon, ice cream, and sauerkraut. Not on the same day, we hope.

Don Gorske of Fond du Lac has outdone both men with a style that's more distance than speed. He has eaten one or two Big Macs every day for more than thirty-five years, and in August 2008 he passed the 23,000 mark. He has kept track ever since May 17, 1972, the day a Big Mac first filled his mouth with joy. Actually he had 9 of them that day (they cost 49 cents then) and 265 in the first month, as he

the lawn just north of the restaurant one day, the terrified goat leaped off the roof, hurdled a parked car, dodged through traffic, jumped into the bay, and started swimming. Al had to chase after it in a boat for the rescue.

discovered when he cleaned out—and counted—the Big Mac pods in the backseat of his car.

Since then he has kept count in little calendar-notebooks (he admits to being a wee bit obsessive), which impressed the Guinness people, who declared him the record holder when he passed the 18,000 mark. (At that point, a math class at a Fond du Lac high school figured out that this number of Big Macs represented 14 beef cattle, 560 pounds of cheese, and 100 gallons of Special Sauce.) But Gorske kept on going because he truly loves Big Macs. Nothing else appeals to him, so every day, after work as a prison guard in Waupun, he goes to McDonald's on Military Road in Fond du Lac for a Big Mac or two. He also has had Big Macs in forty-eight states (and received them by mail from the other two, Alaska and Hawaii); at such U.S. landmarks as the Grand Canyon, Niagara Falls, and Alcatraz Island; and at every major-league baseball stadium, NFL stadium, and NASCAR track in the country.

Gorske is trim—6 feet 2 inches, 179 pounds—and healthy (cholesterol 140). He read in *Newsweek* that McDonald's defense attorneys had invoked him at trial in an obesity lawsuit brought by plaintiffs who must have been chasing their Big Macs with 32-ounce triple-thick shakes. Over the years he has missed only eight days of Big Macs, sometimes because of travel (incredibly, no golden arches appeared on the landscape) or blizzards—he'd have been there, but the place was closed.

Today four or six goats munch away up there, while diners below select from a more interesting menu, starting with Swedish pancakes with lingonberries for breakfast. Al Johnson's Swedish Restaurant is open 6:00 a.m. to 8:00 p.m. Monday through Saturday and 7 a.m. to 8 p.m. Sunday. It's located on Bay Shore Drive (Highway 42). Call (920) 854-2626 or visit www.aljohnsons.com for more information.

The Smithsonian's Loss

Sister Bay

The Dish Museum may run off with the Spoon Museum, but that still leaves the Cup Museum in beautiful little Sister Bay in Wisconsin's Door Peninsula. (No, there is no Door Museum, but I'll mention it to somebody.)

Treasures and trash—sometimes there's a fine line, but not here at the Back Door Studio, where the former Mike Bjorn's Fine Clothing and Museum of Kenosha exhibit of celebrity Styrofoam cups is now enshrined. These are not just any cups, but cups from WGN Chicago radio's Spike O'Dell collection, including the John Hancock of everybody from Harry Caray to Henry Kissinger, Jane Fonda to Dan Quayle, Paul Burrell (Princess Diana's former butler) to Janet Waldo (the voice of Judy Jetson and Fred Flintstone's battle-ax mother-in-law), not to mention former Governor Rod Blagojevich, Mayor Richard Daley, President Jimmy Carter, Senator John McCain, Marie Osmond, Lucie Arnaz, Jim Lehrer, Kitty Kelley, Olympia Dukakis, Tony Randall, a whole disappointing and disappeared squad of Chicago Cubs, and maybe a hundred others, all of whom agreed to sign their cups to get away from Spike.

Previously the collection was in Beloit at Austin's Barber Shop, where hundreds of visitors piled out of tour buses and the lines stretched out the door, after it was at Mike Bjorn's, because a collection like this has to stay on the move. But now it's at home in Door County, a felicitous choice in view of all the Chicagoans hunkering down up there. The collection is priceless and worthless at the same time, says Don Thompson, whose breads, European-style pastries, and

Port des Morts chocolate cake are the other draws at the Door County Bakery; the Cup Museum next door is just icing on the cake.

The bakery and the Back Door Studio are south of Sister Bay on Highway 57 between Settlement Road and Highway Q. Open 8:00 a.m. to 5:00 p.m. Tuesday through Saturday, 8:00 a.m. to 3:00 p.m. Sunday and Monday; closed Tuesday and Wednesday off season. Call (920) 854-1137 or (888) 392-7323, or visit www.doorcountybakery.com

Tootie Loves Chuck
Two Rivers

Two Rivers is the birthplace of both the ice-cream sundae and Charlton Heston's wife. A re-creation of the soda fountain where Edward Berner first poured chocolate sauce over ice cream in 1881 is among

That's Using Your Cheese

In November 1995 Frank Emmert Jr., a die-hard Green Bay Packers fan, was flying home to Superior from a Packers-Browns game in Cleveland. As he neared Stevens Point, ice caused his single-engine plane to lose power. Just before impact Emmert grabbed the foam-rubber cheesehead he'd worn at the game and buried his face in it. He believes it saved his face and arms from serious injury (though not his ankle), and maybe even his life.

National wire services picked up the story, and before long Emmert was being wheeled onto the set of *The Tonight Show* in a cart that resembled a cheese wedge to tell the story to Jay Leno. Today he still travels with his cheesehead.

★ ★

the exhibits at the old Washington House hotel. Less well known but popular for many years, according to a news story posted here, was a 5-cent float consisting of a tall glass of milk, a scoop of ice cream, and crushed oyster crackers.

In the Sons and Daughters Room is an exhibit devoted to Lydia Clarke Heston, who not only was the wife of the late movie actor Heston, but also is the great-great-granddaughter of Hezekiah Huntington Smith, a founder of Two Rivers. Lydia is pictured in her own acting days and with other swimmers in the Polliwog Club of Washington High School. Her annual Christmas letters to a longtime friend and "all of you back in God's country" are here, too. Signed "Tootie and Chuck," several years' worth of newsy letters, each four or five typewritten pages long, are on display, which include some reminiscences, such as the day in 1944 in Greensboro, North Carolina, when "we went for a stroll amid the blooming spring. We passed a small white church with a flowering cherry tree. We tiptoed inside and an hour later we were Sergeant and Mrs. Charlton Heston." The exhibit also reports Chuck's retirement as president of the National Rifle Association.

The second floor of Washington House is something like a Wisconsin Sistine Chapel. The walls and ceiling are covered with generic pastoral and patriotic scenes that were created by mural artists in 1906 and restored by a conservator in the 1990s. Originally the room was used for dances, plays, and wrestling matches; today it's the site of concerts, lectures, and other community events.

Washington House is 1 block east of the main street in Two Rivers ("T'rivers," as the natives call it) at Seventeenth and Jefferson Streets, across from a large museum of wood-type printing and down the street from a history museum that used to be a convent. Open daily year-round from 9:00 a.m. to 9:00 p.m. May through October; 9:00 a.m. to 5:00 p.m. November through April. Call (920) 793-2490 for more information. T'rivers holds an annual Ice Cream Sundae Thursday in June.

A lawn jockey in Packer gear, on Highway 22 just north of the Columbia County–Marquette County line. ERICA SCHLUETER

'Twas a Month before Christmas . . .

On November 22, 1912, the schooner *Rouse Simmons* set out from the U.P., loaded with thousands of Christmas trees for Chicagoans at the other end of Lake Michigan. Its captain, Herman Schuenemann, had been hauling trees to Chicago for almost three decades and by now was known as Captain Santa. The next day, the schooner was sighted off Kewaunee with its flag at half-mast, a sign of distress. The station at Two Rivers, the next one farther south, was notified and sent a powerboat out into the dark and snowy night, but the *Rouse Simmons* had vanished.

A half century later, as if to compensate for the loss of the *Rouse Simmons*'s cargo, Manitowoc—the next town south of Two Rivers—became the birthplace of the aluminum Christmas tree. Known as the aluminum cookware capital, it was already manufacturing everything from saucepans to siding, so it was not a great stretch for the Aluminum Specialty Company to produce the first Evergleam brand tree, in 1959. An immediate sensation, it was followed by about a million more in the 1960s. Most of them were silver but a few came in colors—even pink. Decorations were hardly necessary, but you could add the Shiny Brite ornaments, or even accessorize with a revolving four-color projector called a Sata Lite (these were the days of the space race), which was the only safe way to light the tree. (Think about it—a string of electric lights on an aluminum tree?) Today you might find an aluminum tree at a yard sale (look for a large dusty box) or on eBay.

In 1971 a scuba diver stumbled upon the *Rouse Simmons* about 8 miles off Two Rivers in 172 feet of water with what was left of thousands of trees in its hold. You can explore it, too—and without getting wet—by going to the underwater video gallery at www.wisconsinshipwrecks.org. It's one of twenty-seven ship-wreck sites off Wisconsin that are listed on the National Register of Historic Places—more than any other state—and hundreds more wrecks lie out there.

Rogers Street Fishing Village, 2010 Rogers Street, Two Rivers, has artifacts from the *Rouse Simmons,* including the ship's wheel. The Milwaukee Yacht Club has its anchor. In 1924 some fishermen found Captain Schuenemann's wallet in their nets and returned it to his family.

The Washington Street Antique Mall in Manito-woc displays aluminum trees at holiday time, including this rare peacock model.

★ ★

Nelsen's Bitters Club
Washington Island

Bartenders everywhere keep a small bottle of bitters on hand for flavoring drinks—Manhattans usually, and then they use only a dash. But Nelsen's Hall orders bitters by the case, having been a world leader in its consumption ever since the days of Prohibition.

It was then that resourceful Tom Nelsen, who had worked in a bitters factory in Europe before coming to Washington Island, licensed his tavern as a drugstore, upon discovering that bitters was classified as a medicine. (A Prussian surgeon and veteran of the Battle of Waterloo had concocted it for the upset stomachs of Simón Bolívar's freedom fighters in Venezuela.) At 44.7 percent alcohol, the equivalent of 90-proof whiskey, bitters became a popular remedy on the island, though for what is still subject to some debate.

In time the extraordinary consumption of bitters prompted a letter of inquiry from the House of Angostura of Trinidad and Tobago ("By Appointment to Her Majesty") to its very best customer—Nelsen's stocks only the Angostura label—and was surprised to learn that residents of a tiny island were drinking it straight. They still do.

The exact content of Angostura bitters is a deep dark secret, but it's a distillation of various tropical herbs, barks, and roots. Tom Nelsen drank a pint a day and lived to almost ninety, a good enough reason for islanders to drop in still for "a tapper and a shot of bitters."

In the 1950s Tom's nephew Gunnar started the Bitters Club, which is still going strong. Every year thousands of people join the club by tossing down a shot of bitters and signing the book. Nelsen's Hall Bitters Pub and Restaurant, open year-round, is on Main Road, about 1.5 miles north of the ferry dock. It celebrated its centennial in 1999, and, by foiling the feds during Prohibition, it is the bar with the longest continuous run in Wisconsin. Call (920) 847-2496 for more information.

Little Iceland

Washington Island is the oldest Icelandic community in the United States, which is one reason that old iconoclast Thorstein Veblen spent summers there from 1908 to 1926, studying and writing and brushing up on his Icelandic. He'd got *The Theory of the Leisure Class* out of his system by that time, but more writing along those lines followed in the secluded cabin he built for himself. Every morning he rowed across Little Lake to chitchat in Icelandic with the Bjarnarssons and pick up fresh milk and butter.

A gigantic nest lies along the Raven Nature Trail of the Northern Highland–American Legion State Forest, near Woodruff. It is one of several surprises along the trail, remnants of an outdoor exhibit by international artists called "Forest Art in Wisconsin." Brenda Baker and Henry Drewal of Madison created the nest. JAMES J. NOVAK

Possibly a Cow Jumping over the Moon?

Most alien craft streaking through Wisconsin are shiny, lighted, wedge-shaped BMWs from Chicago's North Shore, hurtling their crews toward their holiday cabins, but our state is no stranger to craft from somewhere far, far beyond Illinois. In fact, one of the first recorded UFO sightings in America was reported in Eagle on April 14, 1897. A craft "looking like a toy balloon" with red and blue lights hovered near the northern horizon—much amazing Otto Lantz, Dr. Colter, and Will Raiche—before flying on to perplex other communities, including Oconto, Marinette, Darlington, Marshfield, Eau Claire, Kenosha, Madison, Rio, Ripon, and Baraboo (where some skeptics thought it may have had a home base in the Ringling Brothers cosmos).

Dundee Mountain, near the town of Osceola, is a favorite gathering place for those who have seen long, glowing, cigar-shaped or red, triangular hovering objects. They come here hoping for another glimpse—or, in some cases, another proctological examination. Bob Kuehn of Fond du Lac, who attends every year, has seen sixty-five

UFOs over the years, the first being a flying washtub when he was four. Bill Benson, the owner of Benson's Hide-A-Way on Long Lake at Dundee and the man behind UFO Daze, an annual summertime event, believes there have been so many sightings in what he considers Wisconsin's Area 51 (of Roswell, New Mexico, fame) because of either our latitude or longitude. Or perhaps it's for the same reason that the beer makers came: "We also have a lot of good water here." Sightings have occurred regularly in Long Lake since an alien craft followed a farmer plowing in 1948.

Jay Rath, in his book *The W-Files,* cites a Vilas County report of local Joe Simonton's close encounter with a flying saucer "brighter than chrome." It landed in his backyard, disgorging three aliens who served him pancakes that "tasted like cardboard" (which many believe had to be Norwegians bearing lefse). Rath lists several hundred other reported sightings around the state—which, in toto, have got to add up to more than just cabin fever. Belleville and Elmwood (you know, where they planned the UFO landing strip?) both have UFO days, and Bill Benson can fill you in on the latest around Long Lake. The number to call is (920) 533-8219.

3

Southeast

The southeast part *of Wisconsin is the part seen first by people flee-ing Chicago on Interstate 90 on Friday afternoon. Some of them pull over at the first opportunity and check in for the weekend, positioning themselves to be first in line for the trip back home on Sunday. More adventurous ones press on to places that at first must sound positively rustic—Spring Green, New Glarus, Mount Horeb—but turn out to offer some of Wisconsin's best-known curiosities.*

Wisconsin's largest city, Milwaukee, is in the southeast section. With a population of 600,000, the city has described itself as "Chicago sev-eral million people ago"—relatively affordable and maneuverable, right smack on Lake Michigan, and with its fair share of fancy architecture, including a bodacious art museum. Never mind that the curiosities described in this section seem to hearken back to Milwaukee's days of beer and bowling.

The second-largest city is Madison, an island in a sea of reality—if you are to believe the T-shirts—a Brigadoon. It is the capital of Wiscon-sin and the home of the university and—come to think of it—a radio comedy-quiz show with a live audience that broadcasts all over the country on Saturday morning. Talk about your curiosities!

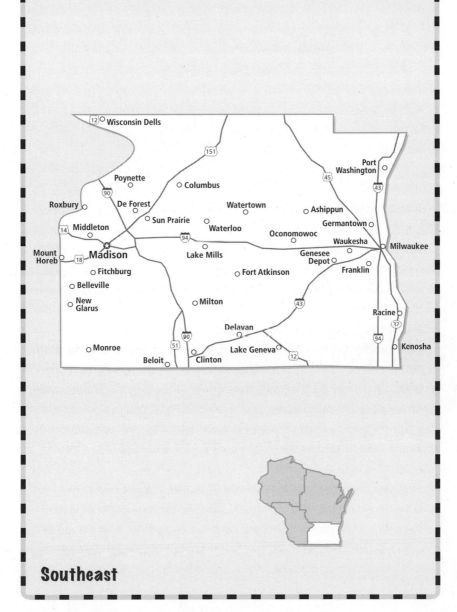

Southeast

★ ★

Honey (That's What I Want)
Ashippun

The Honey Museum asks the question that many bees would ask had they the time: Where would we be without bees?

I'm not saying that our lives would be impoverished without them, but besides all the wonderful pollination work they do, they give us Crayolas, moustache wax, lipstick, teat dilators, Ukrainian Easter-egg designs, and the little sheets you bite down on for the dentist, above and beyond honey. The Egyptians put honey in tombs for life in the hereafter, and Henry VIII signed all his official documents with a bees-wax seal. And that's just two examples.

That's not all, as you shall learn at the museum at Honey Acres. When a bee finds a food source within 50 meters (54 yards), he does the round dance in quick short steps and runs in circles as other bees crowd around. When food is found more than 50 meters away, the bee does the wag-tail dance, and the more rapid the tail wagging, the more exciting the find.

If the food is right on the border between 50 and 50-plus, he does the Watusi.

The statistics are awesome. Honeybees must visit two million flowers to gather enough nectar for one pound of honey. If he thought about it beforehand, he probably wouldn't do it: One bee collects only a tenth of a pound of honey in its entire lifetime, and that goes to the queen. It takes many, many bees flying a total of 25,000 miles to produce one pound of honey—that's equal to once around the world. Let's see sugar say that. How proud we can be of the honeybee, the official state insect.

It takes one Diehnelt family five generations of beekeeping to produce one honey of a museum. It is located 12 miles north of Interstate 94 on Highway 67, 2 miles north of Ashippun. Products are for sale in the shop. Free admission to the museum. Open 9:00 a.m. to 3:30 p.m. Monday through Friday year-round; noon to 4:00 p.m. Saturday and Sunday from May 15 through October 30. Call

★ ★

(920) 474-4411 for tours or more information or visit www.honey acres.com.

Touched by an Exhibit
Beloit

Many of the host of angels at the Angel Museum are made of porcelain or wood, but some are also constructed from drinking straws, tin-can lids, fur, coal, flower petals, or pasta shells (that's a rigatoni body, bow-tie wings, macaroni arms). The angels sing, fly, nap, leapfrog, sew, knit, sweep, fish, marry, jitterbug, and play musical instruments. They wear robes, halos, raincoats, and cheeseheads.

Some function as music boxes, cookie jars, or banks. Some are very small; the second-smallest is an angel-shaped pewter cookie cutter for a dollhouse. There are sets of angels for each day of the week and month of the year. A set of nested angels painted green, pink, and purple is a rarity from Russia. The museum also houses the black angel collection of Oprah Winfrey.

The 6,000 pieces in the museum represent only about half of the collection of Lowell and Joyce Berg. It all began one day in 1976 when they went into an antiques store in Florida and came out with two angel figurines. The following Christmas they noticed several angels among their decorations and decided to collect angels as souvenirs when they traveled. Apparently they traveled a lot, because after that "it just snowballed," says Joyce, who usually wears a silver angel costume with wings as she shows visitors around the museum.

From exit 185 on I-90 (at the landmark 40-foot can of chili with beans at the Hormel plant), go west on Highway 81 for about 3 miles, then turn south at the Rock River and look for the redbrick church with round windows at 656 Pleasant Street. Open 10:00 a.m. to 4:00 p.m. Tuesday through Saturday; also open 1:00 to 4:00 p.m. Sunday, June through August. Closed in January and February. Gift shop. Admission charge. For more information call (608) 362-9099 or go to www .angelmuseum.com.

★ ★

Mark's cool clubhouse. MARK MADSON

A Truck of One's Own

Clinton

About fifteen years ago Mark Madson converted a pickup truck—a 1959 Chevy Fleetside—into a tree house, with help from a buddy with a crane. "For fifteen bucks and a case of beer," says Madson, he hoisted it into a 30-foot tree.

★ ★

What a swell clubhouse it turned out to be! It can hold as many as nine guys for beer and pizza. It's also a secluded spot for a date on Saturday night, if the woman is a good climber.

To keep the weight centered, Mark removed the engine and transmission. He also dumped five tons of dirt around the base of the tree and bolted the truck to the branches. He especially likes being up there in a windstorm. "It kind of creaks," he says. "It's cool because it rocks and rolls." He was there in 1996 when a tornado came through with 60 mph winds that blew the roof off his shed down below. What a ride!

None of this comes as a great surprise to family and friends who remember that when Mark was in seventh grade, he took the engine off a lawn mower, put it in his bicycle, and left home for a week. Over the years many more projects followed. They usually combined engines, something tall, and maybe flames. A few years ago he almost invented the world's biggest weather vane, but it evolved into an artistic auto drop.

The truck in the tree is located 8 miles east of Beloit on the north side of Interstate 43, just before the number 6 exit for Clinton. What Mark does next is anybody's guess. Stay posted at www.harleyheart beat.com.

Wisconsin Discovers Columbus
Columbus

A huge old brick building houses not only Wisconsin's largest antiques mall, but also a museum dedicated to the city's namesake, Christopher Columbus, who, although he never visited Wisconsin, would have liked it here. The large collection of Columbus images includes plates, busts, and posters, in addition to many souvenirs from the World's Columbian Exposition of 1893, which honored his discovery of the New World some 400 years earlier.

The many depictions of the bearded man in mini-bloomers against a backdrop of ocean and ships make it easy to guess what the Exposition's souvenir floaty pens might have looked like. But plastic was not

yet on the horizon, so the souvenirs instead are substantial and sometimes quaint items made of metal, paper, and cloth—thimbles, hairpin
cases, handkerchiefs, watch-case openers, ice-cream molds, and much
more. An especially impressive non sequitur is a $\frac{1}{50}$-scale model of
the world's first Ferris wheel, which debuted at the Exposition. It was
250 feet high (nearly as high as the capitol in Madison), and its brave
passengers rode in thirty-six enclosed cars, sixty in each, for a total
of 2,160 people, many more than the Niña, the Pinta, and the Santa
Maria combined.

An exhibit in the museum's quincentenary department tells the story
of a man who drove 30,000 miles photographing every community in
the United States that was ever named Columbus, even if a tree out
in the middle of a field was all that was left of it. That is the spirit that
settled this great land of ours.

Columbus may be out of favor in many places, but not in
Columbus.

The Columbus Antique Mall and Christopher Columbus Museum,
239 Whitney Street, is about 2 blocks from the center of the business
district. Open 8:15 a.m. to 4:00 p.m. daily. Call (920) 623-1992 for
more information.

You Scratch My Bank

Columbus

In 1919, when more peas were canned in Columbus, Wisconsin, than
anywhere else in the world, the town had something else to brag
about: a bank designed by Louis Sullivan.

The old Farmers and Merchants Union Bank had outlived the tele-
phone building. It was time to build. Naturally the bank president at
first thought along the lines of Greek classical, but for his wife, no
ordinary bank would do. She knew Sullivan's reputation and had seen
photographs of his banks. The "father of the skyscraper" was sum-
moned, he stayed, he designed. He did not express an opinion about

He thought Greek classical, she thought Louis Sullivan.

ERICA SCHLUETER

canned peas. More history and description—tendrils, lintels, and all—are at www.fmub.com/about/history.asp.

The bank caught the eye of movie scouts and now it plays a part in *Public Enemies* (2009), as does Johnny Depp as John Dillinger. Columbus was all atwitter when Universal Studios came to town, even if it meant ripping out the parking meters downtown and replacing the asphalt with rubber cobblestones.

The bank—Sullivan's last work—is at 159 West James Street. The lobby opens at 9:00 a.m. and closes at 3:00 p.m. Monday through Thursday, at 5:30 p.m. Friday, and at 11:00 a.m. Saturday. The mezzanine has a small museum. Call (920) 623-4000 for information.

Cloning Around at ABS
De Forest

ABS (American Breeders Service) Global is known to dairymen worldwide for its leadership in artificial insemination of cattle—and to Wisconsin motorists on I-90/94 for the puns on its billboard at company headquarters (OUR WIT IS A PLAY ON SEMENTICS, explained one).

ABS GENETICS IMPROVE YOUR DAIRY-HEIR. ABS THE CHAMPAGNE OF BOTTLED BULL. ABS IS THE CATTLE-ACT OF THE A.I. INDUSTRY. OUR BEST ASSETS ARE FROZEN. CALL US WHEN YOUR HEIFER'S IN THE MOOED. QUALITY GENETICS—MORE THAN A COWINCIDENT. LET ABS PUT A SMILE ON YOUR COW-TENANTS. MANY ARE CALLED BUT FEW ARE FROZEN. OUR GENES DON'T FADE. WE DELIVER THE MALE. At holiday time, ANGUS WE HAVE HEARD ON HIGH. They just keep coming.

ABS Global is also known for producing the world's first cloned calf (named Gene, of course) in 1997, just six months after Scotland announced the clone of the sheep Dolly (GENETIC PROGRESS IS ALL RELATIVE). By now, ABS has a herd of cloned cows.

ABS was founded in 1941, at first employing the delivery technique pictured on page 123, and the company shows signs of staying in business FOR HEIFER AND HEIFER. In 1999 ABS merged with a British company

The Cow That Roared

We wuz robbed: Wisconsin is only a shadow of its former self.

In a lumber swindle instigated by wealthy New Englanders prior to Wisconsin's admittance to the Union in 1848, the land between the St. Croix and Mississippi Rivers, including some choice parcels known as Minneapolis and St. Paul, a good chunk of northern Illinois ranging from Rock Falls to Chicago, and all of what should be known as the Upper Peninsula of Wisconsin, were stripped away from the state. We coulda been a contender, rivaling California and New York in electoral votes and general clout.

The insult to Badger pride was so great that Wisconsin actually seceded from the Union in 1843, only nobody noticed. Under the dotty James Doty, territorial governor, Wisconsin declared itself to be a sovereign and independent (and thereby eligible for foreign aid) state ready to defend its integrity and citizenry—in effect, declaring war on the United States of America. This remains the only American war in which no skirmishes were fought, unless it was the one in Congress that caused Doty to be transferred to Utah, where it was thought he could do little harm. As in the South, some resentment remains to this day.

to form the largest artificial-insemination company in the world. WITH ABS MORE PROFIT IS IN THE BAG.

The bullboard is on the east side of I-90/94 between Highway V (exit 126) and Highway 19 (exit 131). For more bovine news, see www.abs global.com.

★ ★

Romeo and Juliet
Delavan

Delavan was the home of twenty-six different circus companies in the 1800s, and the elephant that stands on a monument downtown in Tower Park is a facsimile of a rogue elephant, Romeo, who lived here between 1854 and 1865. One of the largest Indian elephants ever exhibited in America, he stood nearly 11 feet tall and weighed 10,500 pounds. In his day Romeo crushed, tusked, trampled, or otherwise killed five handlers. One time he escaped from his barn and terrorized the area for three days until captured.

An elephant named Juliet was from the same herd, imported from Ceylon (modern-day Sri Lanka) in 1851 for the P. T. Barnum Asiatic Caravan. Juliet was as delightful as Romeo was dangerous. She pulled a bandwagon in street parades, performed in the ring, and generally charmed her trainers.

Because she died in the month of February, in 1864, when the ground was frozen, Juliet's body was weighted down and deposited through a large rectangular hole sawed in the ice of Lake Delavan. In May 1897 a man trolling for northern pike off Lake Lawn reeled in part of a rib cage thought to have belonged to Juliet, and in 1931 a drag-line operation yielded a tibia. Presumably the rest of her bones are still at the bottom of the lake.

Romeo died in Chicago in 1892 after surgery for a foot infection, but the month was June, the weather was warm, and his remains were disposed of in the municipal dumping grounds.

Dairy Shrine/Hoard Museum
Fort Atkinson

William Dempster Hoard taught the gospel of dairy farming. The National Dairy Shrine, adjacent to the Hoard Historical Museum, exhibits such relics as cow clippers, tail holders, glass milk bottles with their little cardboard lids, butterfat testers, cream separators, and even a dog-powered butter churn.

Artificial insemination of cattle used to be a chancy business. Sometimes the parachute that delivered the goods, like this one at the National Dairy Shrine, blew into the next county.

Representing modern technology is a photo exhibit that details today's method of artificial insemination of dairy cattle, from collection to next generation. It makes another item on display seem especially touching: the parachute that dropped semen from the air to breeders down below before the advent of frozen semen. It looks like a little silk parasol, and its precious package is wrapped in discreet plain brown

★ ★

paper. A photograph of a very small plane, the *Flying Bull,* and its barnstorming pilot completes the picture.

The Hoard Historical Museum has artifacts from the Black Hawk War; hundreds of arrowheads handsomely displayed; many mounted birds, including a passenger pigeon; and a horse-skin rug with mane.

Located on Whitewater Avenue (Highway 12 East) in Fort Atkinson. Open 9:30 a.m. to 3:30 p.m. Tuesday through Saturday from Labor Day to Memorial Day; 9:30 a.m. to 4:30 p.m. Tuesday through Saturday and 11:00 a.m. to 3:00 p.m. Sunday from Memorial Day to Labor Day. No hours on Monday, ever. Call (920) 563-7769 for details or visit www.hoardmuseum.org.

Ten Chimneys
Genesee Depot

For decades Alfred Lunt and Lynn Fontanne were America's "First Couple" of the theater, and when they finished a long run on Broadway they came home to Genesee Depot. Here they could roam the fields or play host to all their theatrical friends. Helen Hayes stayed here for a month or so every year. Eugene O'Neill worked on *Strange Interlude.* Noel Coward played the piano (and painted pictures all over it). Many others came and went—Charlie Chaplin, Laurence Olivier, Carol Channing, Katharine Hepburn, Julie Harris, Alexander Woollcott, S. N. Behrman, Robert Sherwood, Moss Hart—all right here in the rural hamlet of Genesee Depot.

Lunt had grown up in Milwaukee and loved the Wisconsin countryside. Over the years he acquired land, converted a chicken coop into a summer cottage, and added buildings whose chimneys numbered ten and gave the estate its name. Lunt was serious about his land. He grew strawberries, raspberries, tomatoes, cucumbers, turnips, potatoes, and corn. He made his own butter and bred cattle.

"The Fabulous Lunts" designed every room in the main house like a stage set, fit for grand entrances and exits. A set designer covered the walls and ceilings with elaborate murals. In one scene from the

Old Testament, Adam and Eve resemble each other because Fontanne posed for both. Fond of old things, she said, "Being in a modern house all the rest of my life would be just like sitting nude forever in the center of a huge white dinner plate." Artwork and antiques from New York and Europe fill the rooms.

Lunt and Fontanne were married for fifty-five years. Lunt died in 1977, and Fontanne stayed on at Ten Chimneys until she died in 1983.

Rick Serocki sawed a purple 1955 Fleetwood Cadillac in half and planted it in his front yard in Cudahy. Its bumper sticker says IF WE CAN'T FIX IT, WE'LL BURY IT—MILWAUKEE BODY SHOP. A seven-foot Big Boy stands on the garage roof.
RICK SEROCKI

Can I Use Your Carmex?

The garage in Franklin, Wisconsin, where alchemist Alfred Woelbing first concocted Carmex in a ceramic warlock's pot has been demolished, but you can still tour the plant to watch molten lip balm poured into the diminutive white jars of mythic proportions. You just can't get too close to the production line, as the secrets of the process are a closely held family secret. Woelbing was the active president of the company until 2001, when he died at the age of one hundred (perhaps Carmex cures the ravages of age as well as cold sores). His son and grandsons continue the company tradition.

While many believe that Carmex use caused the sixties, it really was invented in 1936 and may therefore have caused the thirties, forties, and fifties as well (although the Second World War disrupted grease availability, the core of the product). Carmex, perhaps because of comedian Paula Poundstone's "Carmex addict" routines, is reported to contain an addictive agent (some suggest fiberglass or an acid that causes an itch continually needing to be soothed), but Carmex dismisses any such myths at its Web site, www.carma-labs.com.

Since 1987 Carmex has also come in little tubes, but it's just not the same. Long-term addicts claim the mere sound of the tiny jar opening provides relief from a host of symptoms, including but not limited to chapped derma.

It had been their permanent home since 1972, their summer retreat since the 1920s.

In 2003, after a multimillion-dollar restoration, Ten Chimneys was opened to the public as a museum and arts center. Tours are offered Tuesday through Saturday, May through mid-November. Admission charge. Call (262) 968-4110 for reservations. Its Web address is www.tenchimneys.org.

Flossie's Best Friend

If Wisconsin does have more cows than people, it is only because they are encouraged to breed. And encouraging them to breed is the legacy of William D. Hoard of Fort Atkinson. Hoard was one of the first to speak of "cow temperament," something the rest of us in Dairyland have come to take for granted as a birthright.

Around the turn of the last century, Hoard wrote the dairy commandments:

• Speak to a cow as you would to a lady.

• Remember that a cow is a mother and her calf is a baby.

• To him that loveth a cow, shall all other things be added—feed, ensilage, butter, more grasses, more prosperity, happier homes and greater wealth.

Hoard promoted the radical notions of the single-purpose milker, the building of silos, and the testing of milk to protect against tuberculosis and, in fact, transformed the farm in which several cows were kept into the modern dairy industry and the landscape of Wisconsin into the beautiful patchwork of dairy farms and fields you see today. Along the way he served in the Civil War; was elected governor of the state (as a Republican and Lincoln disciple, although ridiculed as the "cow candidate"); promoted the planting of alfalfa; brought ag science to the University of Wisconsin; made the farmer a political force to be reckoned with nationally; and founded *Hoard's Dairyman,* the influential journal still published today.

A statue of Hoard stands at the head of the agricultural campus at the University of Wisconsin–Madison, where you will want to be sure to stop at Babcock Hall to sample the ice cream and visit the dairy barns.

★ ★

Bells Bells Bells Bells Bells Bells Bells
Germantown

Bells for horses, sheep, water buffalo, elephants, turkeys, dogs, babies, sleighs, bikes, and the Salvation Army. Bells that look like turtles, sea-horses, Santa Claus, Charlie Chaplin, King Arthur, Little Miss Muffett, and Clara Barton. Bells made of brass, pottery, bisque, copper. Bells from every country. Bell-things that dial rotary phones in India and bells that signal a fisherman that he's got a bite. Bells for more reasons than you ever imagined. Even hell's bells might be here.

The bells belonged to Sila Lydia Bast, who grew up nearby and found her first bell, a cowbell, in a field not far from here. She started a collection and word got around. When she worked with her family at the Little Gem Restaurant in Milwaukee, customers brought her bells. Later she became a world traveler and collected more bells. The bells started to add up. Before all was said and done, the Swiss had cast a cowbell especially in her honor. Talk about your tintinnabulation!

Bast Bell Museum is 2 miles east of Highway 41/45 (Holy Hill Road exit). Open 1:00 to 4:00 p.m. Wednesday through Sunday, April through October, year-round by appointment. Admission charge. Call (262) 628-3170 or visit www.bastbellmuseum.com. Before you leave, take a look in the next room at a very spiffy 1929 fire truck.

Trivia

In 1910 Cooper Underwear Company patented its Kenosha Klosed Krotch long underwear, and the following year it became the first underwear manufacturer to advertise in national magazines. In 1972 the Kenosha company changed its name to Jockey International. Its world headquarters remain in Kenosha.

In about 1862, when John Muir was a student at the University of Wisconsin, he invented a desk that awoke him by collapsing his bed and lighting a lamp. The desk gave him a few minutes to get dressed, and then it opened the first book he planned to study, whisked it away at the allotted time, opened the next book, and kept this up until he'd read all his assignments. The desk is about 9 feet tall, has legs whittled into the shapes of little books, and is on display on the main floor of the Wisconsin Historical Society in Madison. John Muir became famous as a naturalist and conservationist. WISCONSIN HISTORICAL SOCIETY

★ ★

A flying saucer at rest on County Highway D north of Belleville, where several UFO sightings were reported in the 1970s. This one has a hatchway and running lights. ERICA SCHLUETER

Gawking and Walking
Lake Geneva

Lake Geneva is one of the few places in the country that still delivers mail by boat, and the boat seems to be the only one that invites passengers to come aboard and watch the show. See the postal person leap off the boat, scamper across the pier, shove the mail in the box, race back with the outgoing mail in her teeth, and leap onto the rail of the 75-foot *Walworth II,* which never stopped! Everybody cheers!

But there's more. Those piers are attached not to cottages but to grandiose estates. As you shall hear (between deliveries, the mail jumper demonstrates that she can read fast, too), many of these mansions were built by captains of Chicago-area industries: brewing, chewing gum, meat packing, railroads, department stores, hotels, pianos, bicycles, washing machines—everything from salt to barbed wire. Who'd have thought there was so much money in paper caps for milk bottles? A lot, if you invented them, as Olaf Tevander did and then retired to that chalet-style mansion at age twenty-six. (You may remember seeing his bottle caps at the National Dairy Shrine, page 123).

Then there's Otto Young's place. He started out selling jewelry from a pushcart and ended up building the largest house on the lake, approximately the size of Xanadu. Another imposing manor was built under a circus tent so that A. C. Bartlett—that old sweetie!—could surprise his wife on her birthday. The estate called Black Point is open for tours to those willing and able to climb the hundred steps that stand between the pier and the house.

Curiosities along the way include a four-story guesthouse that's a fully operational lighthouse, a la the Cape Elizabeth Light in Maine. The occupants of the house on Duck Island have to park at the country club and complete the commute by golf cart.

If you want to check out the architecture, the landscaping, or the lamp in the picture window at closer range, you can take a walk-and-gawk self-tour, which allows you to tromp right across the front lawns of these grand estates. The property is private, but the path is public. Note that the yard art tends more toward iron ibis than plastic flamingo, and the lawn furniture . . . but, hey, the chairs I bought at Target look as good as those! Hear the pooka-pooka of their tennis balls in the distance. Mostly the occupants are invisible—probably inside, writing checks.

The mail boat departs at 10:00 a.m. daily, mid-June through October, from Riviera Docks, a block south of the main downtown intersection

A mail jumper in action. WISCONSIN DEPARTMENT OF TOURISM

of Broad Street (Highway 120) and Main Street (Highway 50) in Lake Geneva (the town). The trip around Geneva Lake (the lake) lasts about two and a half hours. Admission charge; reservations recommended. For more information see www.cruiselakegeneva.com. To purchase the Geneva Lake Shore Path guide, called *Walk, Talk, and Gawk*, go to www.walktalkgawk.com. It includes maps, breaks down the 21-mile path into seven segments, and offers highlights and history.

A Pyramid Scheme?
Lake Mills

Lake Mills owes its nickname, "City of Pyramids" (and such local businesses as the Pyramid City Driving School), to three mysterious shapes at the bottom of Rock Lake.

In the nineteenth century Winnebagoes were telling the early European settlers of Lake Mills about sunken "rock tepees," and one day in 1900 two local duck hunters peered down and saw them. Over the years fishermen and divers have reported sighting something—and described an upside-down ice-cream cone, or a Hershey's Chocolate Kiss, 20 or 30 feet high and 100 feet long—but most of the time water conditions have defied even high-tech video equipment. Are they man-made or glacial debris? Some believe that pre-Columbian dwellers built them on dry land before the area was flooded. Others say that geology can explain the whole thing. The question remains: archaeological find of the century, or nature at work?

Those in the pyramid-builder camp point to large, flat-topped pyramidal mounds a few miles east of Lake Mills. Archaeologists say that the people who lived here between about A.D. 900 and 1200 built the mounds, plus a stockade of wooden posts around their village. One mound had fire pits lined with sand; another was for burials; a third was used for storing corn. Portions of the stockade and two mounds have been reconstructed at Aztalan State Park.

The unexplained underwater shapes are at the south end of Rock Lake. The archaeological site is within Aztalan State Park and is listed on the National Register of Historic Places. The park is located south of I-94 (exit 259) and is open daily. For more information call (608) 873-9695.

Ancient Fossils in the Capitol
Madison

The yellow marble walls of the Hearing Room in the State Capitol Building contain dozens of ammonites, from the days when the future capitol site was sunk in a seventy-million-year-old sea and giant snails made backroom deals. (The ancient fossils look just like big snails.)

You don't have to wait for a hearing on some burning issue to see them. Most of the time the Hearing Room is unoccupied, and you're welcome to go in and look around. The ammonites are at eye level, and some of them are as large as 8 inches across.

When you leave the Hearing Room, head down the right side of the grand staircase and admire the starfish fossil on the fourth step from the bottom. It's about 400 million years old, and geologists say it's extremely rare. (Starfish lack the rigid skeleton necessary for preservation as fossils.)

At the bottom of the staircase, bear right toward the west wing and walk down the grand staircase to the ground floor. To the right of the bottom step is a cephalopod, about 20 inches long. This creature is also about 400 million years old; it lived in the sea, and, like the ammonite, had a hard body but a straight one, not coiled. You can see the breathing tube that ran down the length of its shell—it inhaled to sink, exhaled to rise. If you cross the rotunda to the south wing, you can see another cephalopod, or a chunk of one, on the floor between the two drinking fountains near the elevator on the east side.

The Hearing Room is in the north wing, second floor. Free guided tours of this glorious building are offered daily. Large groups should make an online reservation at www.wisconsin.gov/state/captour or call (608) 266-0382. On a scale of one to ten, say State Capitol junkies, this one is an eleven.

Eau de Corpse
Madison

What's huge and smelly and looks like a giant penis? No wonder *Amorphophallus* (that's where the phallus comes in) *titanum* (aka Titan Arum, corpse flower) draws crowds. The stench may be overwhelming, but it's nice to view an attraction and not have the smell of rotting flesh be your own. When this Audrey Jr. opens, it's special, or so the thousands filing past to pay their respects at the University of Wisconsin botany greenhouse think. Giant flies and a super beetle were attracted, too, on this particular morning of June 9, 2005, a bit early even for old Up and Arum. Back in Indonesia they are known to sleep in. In Jakarta, it is said, when the corpse flower blooms, it is time to move on.

The beautiful beast blooms at the botany greenhouse. M. FAYYAZ

Titan Arum was, at this very rare moment in June, blooming in the botany greenhouse at the University of Wisconsin, which stayed open past midnight—who could sleep? Besides, the smell is stronger at night, and it takes a heady whiff to attract hordes of tourists, graduate students, and flower club ladies looking for a walk on the wild side. The process of blooming is intense and lasts only a few days, but boy, oh boy, is it worth it. At full glory, when the flower looks like Penis on a Half-Shell, Titan Arum extends itself to a full 10 feet, its maroon head unfurling to 3 or 4 feet across. Before you know it, say seventy-two hours, it's over.

Two of UW's several Titan Arums bloomed in June 2005, and one of those bloomed—for the third time—again in 2008. It's hard to predict when blooms will occur. They do not seem to be aware of each other, and cross-pollination is strictly discouraged since who wants a fruit that size? Generally a cultivated Titan Arum (and some of them are, you know) blooms only three or four times in its forty-year lifetime, and leaves the house not at all. UW botanists may be doing a corpse flower mating dance for their specimens, however, since three plants have bloomed at least twice in recent years. We'll have to check their potting soil!

If you are a lover of big stinky things, you owe it to yourself to drop whatever you're doing when you hear that Titan's about to unleash, and get yourself over here. If you can't make it to Madison, check out www.botany.wisc.edu, which provided live Titan video streaming in past years. If you're a glutton for stinky, you can read even more fascinating details about the eau du corpse at http://botit.botany.wisc.edu/Titan_Arum_Archive/index.html.

* *

The King Steps In
Madison

Thirty years had gone by and the Wisconsin Historical Society still had not planted a historical marker at the site of one of the milestones in Madison's rich history. Around the state more than 500 markers inform travelers about important events in Wisconsin's past (or would if they'd pull over and stop long enough to read)—the Black Hawk War, the Peshtigo Fire, Colby cheese—but here, nothing.

Finally, in 2007, Suburban Wheels stepped forward and placed a large granite plaque at the corner of Highway 51 and East Washington Avenue. The inscription is entitled "Elvis Presley Fight Scene":

> On this site, around 1 a.m., on June 24, 1977, Elvis Presley was riding in the second of two limousines which had stopped for a red light. He was coming from a concert in Des Moines and had just arrived in Madison. Elvis noticed a young teen on the ground being beaten by two other youths here at the former Skyland Service Station. Elvis jumped out of his limo and moved quickly to the fight scene. They admitted later that they knew it was the legendary Elvis Presley who was standing in front of them in his classic karate stance saying, "I'll take you on." After a few classic karate moves by Elvis, the youths recognized him, stood and shook hands, and promised to stop fighting. Elvis asked, "Is everything settled now?" Elvis was on his way to the Sheraton and his last Madison appearance. He died 52 days later, on August 16, 1977.

The plaque was dedicated on the thirtieth anniversary of Presley's death. Three scuffling youths reenacted the fight, a limo pulled up to the curb, and an Elvis impersonator stopped the fight. The crowd snacked on collector's edition Reese's Peanut Butter and Banana Crème candy, the King's favorite flavor combo, and "Love Me Tender" played on the PA system.

The plaque is at the busy intersection of Stoughton Road (Highway 51) and East Washington Avenue, on the Suburban Wheels corner, where the Skyland station used to be.

★ ★

This grove of asparagus stalks appeared overnight at the entrance to Forest Hill Cemetery in Madison, another in a series from a mystery artist.

Entomologizer and Cricket Spitter
Madison

Dan Capps holds the world's record in cricket spitting. First he won the Bug Bowl Cricket-Spitting Contest at Purdue University, where he was exhibiting his insect collection. Then, to satisfy Guinness's tough standards, he repeated the deed on its *World Records Prime Time* television show in Hollywood. His official distance is 32 feet ½ inch.

A competition cricket is dead, limp, and mushy, having been frozen and thawed.

Dan's personal insect collection contains tens of thousands of insects—wasps, beetles, moths, butterflies, dragonflies, and, of course,

The Dreamkeepers, two 35-foot birds, offer a unique landmark for the occupants of 211 South Paterson in Madison. They were created by Dr. Evermor of Baraboo (see page 178), who loves birds "because they are the most nonthreatening species on our planet." As usual, he used industrial scrap: parts from a semi that tipped over in Indiana, two large blowers, and many scissors blades. The Dreamkeepers have intergalactic names: Yon and Beyond. JIM WILDEMAN

crickets—with an emphasis on tropical species. It's an enormous collection for an amateur (he earned his livelihood as a mechanic at Oscar Mayer), and it has been displayed at the Museum of Science and Industry in Chicago. Dan's knowledge of insects is self-taught, and he often shows and talks about wonders of the insect world at schools and elsewhere. (His own fascination with insects began in grade school

Jeffersonian Democracy

Thomas Jefferson never made it to Wisconsin (although his exploratory committee—Lewis, Clark, and Sacagawea—made it darn close). But his youngest son by Sally Hemings, his household slave at Monticello, did.

Eston Hemings Jefferson is buried in Madison's Forest Hills cemetery (on Speedway Road), along with his wife, Julia, and eight family members. Eston was the scion of a successful and well-respected Madison family that ran the Capital Hotel, a livery business that was active in early union associations. Recently DNA testing provided evidence that Eston's father was one of the Founding Fathers. Jefferson never formally freed his slaves, but purportedly agreed to allow many to run away.

In 1836, at age twenty-eight, Eston fled to Ohio, and when the political tide turned against former slaves with the passage of the Fugitive Slave Act, he moved to the freshly minted state of Wisconsin in 1851. He married a black woman but lived as a white man, concealing his family history to his death in 1856. His brother Madison, who lived in Ohio, claimed the lineage to Jefferson in a biography and mentioned a brother in Wisconsin, though not by name, for his brother's well-being.

after the principal saw Dan running around with a butterfly net, called him to his office, opened a cigar box, and showed Dan his luna and cecropia moths.) Dan sees his school visits as a chance to open eyes to diversity in nature and to enlighten—people who shriek at the sight of an insect the size of a baseball, for instance, learn that large insects often are harmless. A well-respected collector, he also addresses ento-mologists' professional meetings.

Dan's own person further testifies to the significance of ecology in his life. Two artist friends designed a tapestry of images from nature— his favorite butterflies, insects, and flowers—that is tattooed over his upper body (but it doesn't extend below his elbows; that is, the tat-too insects won't freak out the school principal at his "Introduction to Insects" visits at grade schools).

The 27-foot Wienermobile has a hot dog–shaped glove box and instrument panel, relish-colored seats, and stor-age space for up to 10,000 wiener whistles. Drivers of the six-wiener fleet are usually recent college graduates who must train at Hot Dog High in Madison, the home of Oscar Mayer Foods, before they get the keys to the five-ton wiener. COURTESY KF HOLDINGS, INC.

Good Grief

Middleton

Sam Sanfillippo displays his enormous collection of taxidermied wildlife downstairs at the funeral home that bears his name. It takes four rooms to exhibit the hundreds of fish, birds, and animals he has bagged or landed or otherwise acquired, and there are more at home. As a teenager he caught the gigantic marlin on the wall, which is almost eclipsed by all that followed.

He and his personal Northwoods taxidermist have had loads of fun dreaming up settings for all this wildlife. At the "Woodland Fair," several chipmunks ride a merry-go-round, while others in skirts of gold upholstery fringe perform at the "topless girlie show." Gray squirrels line up for refills at a Northwoods bar. Four chipmunks play cards, one

Last call before bar time at the funeral home.

★ ★

kibitzes. The squirrel at the piano wears tiny earphones. Albino squirrels shoot baskets at a Fisher-Price hoop or cruise in pink convertibles.

Not cast in roles but also on display are curiosities just playing themselves: a three-legged goose, blonde raccoons, fetal fawns, a paddle-nosed catfish.

Photographs of Sanfillippo with presidents, governors, and astronauts offer another dimension of his long, full life. And the animals speak for themselves.

Visitors are welcome, but call first: (608) 238-8406. Fitch-Lawrence-Sanfillippo-Cress Funeral Home is at 6021 University Avenue.

A Secret Tunnel
Milton

Joseph Goodrich was an innkeeper, a devout Seventh Day Baptist, and such a staunch abolitionist that he dug a 50-foot tunnel between his log cabin and his inn to aid fugitive slaves as they traveled the Underground Railroad to freedom. When runaways found their way to the cabin, Goodrich lifted the secret trapdoor to the secret tunnel that led to the secret room in the basement. There they could hide and rest up for the next leg of the perilous journey.

The Underground Railroad of the nineteenth century was not, of course, a real railroad, and this seems to be the only part of it that actually was underground.

The inn was Milton House, and upstairs from the secret room, guests were resting up after a hard day's stagecoach ride. Sojourner Truth was once a guest, and although she and Goodrich saw eye to eye on abolition, they disagreed on smoking. Sojourner Truth smoked a pipe, and Goodrich told her that she wouldn't get to heaven because smoking made her breath bad. She said she wouldn't need her breath in heaven.

Goodrich was one of Milton's first settlers (and therefore didn't have to worry about neighbors who might wonder why he was digging that tunnel), having arrived in March 1839 with his family after a thirty-four-day trip by covered wagon from Alfred, New York—a

hotbed of the abolitionist movement. He constructed the inn in 1844, and when it was finished, the *Janesville Gazette* described it as "truly an object of curiosity." It was in the shape of a hexagon and had a chimney in the middle so that each room could have its own stove and stovepipe connection to the chimney.

In 1998 the National Park Service officially recognized the Milton House Museum as a National Historic Landmark for its role in the Underground Railroad. The museum is located at the intersection of Highways 26 and 59. Guided tours daily from 10:00 a.m. to 5:00 p.m. Memorial Day through Labor Day and weekends in May (tours by arrangement at other times of year). Admission charge. Call (608) 868-7772 or visit www.miltonhouse.org for more information.

Polka Values
Milwaukee

Art Altenburg felt safe in saying that Art's Concertina Bar was the only concertina bar in the U.S.A. For twenty-five years Art and his concertina collection constituted a concertina universe. (It's like an accordion, with buttons instead of keys.) Polka bands like Karl and the Country Dutchmen from Minnesota came on weekends, and hundreds showed up to dance and yell "hey" every four bars or so. Sometimes Art serenaded the crowd with his own "Oof Oof Polka."

But when the time came to retire in 2007, Art packed up most of his concertinas and sold the place to Andy Kochanski, a native South Sider who respects polka values. Oh, Andy changed a few things; for instance, he added a Bonzini foosball table and repealed Art's no-accordions law. Occasionally he challenges patrons to cross the New Frontier into other musical genres—though never, ever heavy metal—but overall, polka prevails.

There are live polka bands from 8:00 to midnight on weekends; polka jam sessions on Wednesday night; polka lessons (it's really not hard), as well as waltz and fox-trot, on Thursday night. Sometimes more polkaing on Sunday afternoon. So, no need to wait for Polka

★ ★

Trivia

Grout fanciers may be interested to know that Milton House is the oldest poured-grout structure in the United States.

Fest downtown in June when Kochanski's Concertina Beer Hall is at it year-round. Like Art's, it's still a destination, a field trip, a quintessential experience for locals and tourists who want to check out the polka bar on the South Side.

Kochanski's Concertina (in honor of the past) Beer (for the selection of Polish, German, and Wisconsin brews) Hall, 1920 South Thirty-seventh Street, off Burnham Avenue, is open from 2:00 p.m. to bar time Tuesday through Sunday. For information call (414) 837-6552 (83-POLKA) or visit www.beer-hall.com.

And Some Really Ancient Pin Boys

Milwaukee

From the outside Holler House looks like about a thousand other corner taverns in Milwaukee, but beyond the door at the end of the bar and down the stairs is bowling history: the oldest alleys (all two of them) in the nation.

The American Bowling Congress sanctioned them in 1910, and they're very much in use today. See the bowling bags lined up in the "locker room"—two long shelves under the front window. Some regulars have been coming for forty years.

Bowlers sacrifice fifteen or twenty points to play here. It's disorienting to bowl in a tunnel instead of a thirty-lane alleyrama, on hardwood instead of synthetic lanes, with balls that come rumbling back in full view from human pin setters busily scampering around back there.

Photos of bowling teams confirm the history—upstanding-looking guys wearing white shirts and neckties and representing Ryczek Embalmers, Miller High Life, La Dora Cigars. Fourth-generation owner Marcy Skowronski knows the neighborhood stories that go with them. She also can explain another feature of the Holler House decor: brassieres autographed by their owners, dangling in bunches from various fixtures throughout the tavern.

Holler House, 2042 West Lincoln, opens for business at 4:00 p.m. every day except Monday. Call to inquire about bowling (414-647-9284), and watch for scenes filmed at Holler House in the movie *Chump Change*.

Not a bird, not a plane—but the Milwaukee Art Museum, as if ready to flap its wings and take off across Lake Michigan. Architect Santiago Calatrava designed the Quadracci Pavilion with wings forming a sunshade that opens and closes when the museum opens and closes (10:00 a.m. to 5:00 p.m. daily, until 8:00 on Thursday), and also at noon. Details at www.mam.org. WISCONSIN DEPARTMENT OF TOURISM (TIMOTHY HURSLEY)

Milwaukee Talking

In Milwaukee "Come by the house later" does not mean that the speaker is expecting you to make an offer on the duplex, nor does it imply that the addressee will not be invited in. It's just how you ask somebody over. Though if you can't wait to be asked, you can still station yourself under a friend's window and yell "Call for Steve-ee!" if, in fact, it's Stevie you want to see.

Milwaukee's German argot (further complicated in my family with Yiddish-isms) makes "bubblers" out of drinking fountains, finds "ice-box" still the preferred term for refrigerator, and "ain'a?" the way to conclude a declarative sentence. ("Follow me?" my dad's preferred closer, is another favorite.)

While it may not be true that Milwaukee nearly entered the war on the German side, "Cream City" syntax owes a lot to loose—or literal—translations from the German and, on the South Side, the Polish. *Milwaukee Talk,* a pamphlet originally published by the *Milwaukee Journal* in the 1950s (and cited in James P. Leary's *Wisconsin Folklore*) is an invaluable primer for wannabe Milwaukeeans:

- "It's warm in here. Why don't you run up the window?"
- "From the refrigerator get the eggs and I will fry you."
- "Don't nervous me, I get easy mad."
- "Come broom off the snow, the sidewalk is getting thick."
- "I gotta clean my hairs, they're so greasy."

Naturally, to poetry it lends itself:

I give to you a violet
In token of I'm glad we met
I hope we may already yet
Once more again together got.

This house was built in 1926 from plans for a ship, by a salesman who dreamed of sailing the high seas. White with blue trim and with a 30-foot lighthouse off the starboard bow, the one-bedroom *Edmund B* is at 3138 North Cambridge Avenue (at East Hampshire Street), near the University of Wisconsin–Milwaukee campus. ERICA SCHLUETER

One summer day in 1909, Ole Evinrude purchased ice cream for a picnic, but by the time he rowed across Okauchee Lake in Waukesha County to the picnic, it had melted. His disappointment led to his inventing "the detachable rowboat motor" and organizing Evinrude Motor Company.
JIM LEGAULT

The tin man of Highway 78 awaits his friend the rural letter carrier. Farther down the driveway is 13-foot-high Peg Leg Pete, a pirate with rail spikes for teeth and a frying pan for an eye patch. Created by Wally Keller and located about halfway between Black Earth and Mount Horeb.
ERICA SCHLUETER

Why Milwaukee Feels Badly

John Schrank, a bartender, convinced that Theodore Roosevelt intended to establish a monarchy by running for a third term, stalked him for 2,000 miles before putting a bullet in him in Milwaukee in 1912. It didn't help that William McKinley had appeared to him in a dream pointing to Roosevelt as McKinley's murderer—which, in Schrank's mind, was more portentous than just something he had eaten before retiring.

Fortunately for Roosevelt, the length of his speech may have saved his life. The bullet had to pass through the doubled-up bulk of a fifty-page speech as well as a case for the metal spectacles he needed to read it. In true Bull Moose fashion, he railed for an hour with the bullet lodged 5 inches into his chest, where, having missed all major organs and arteries, it was to remain for the rest of his life. Roosevelt said, "I don't want Milwaukee to feel badly about this," which has come to be the city's unofficial motto since October 14,

Remember to First Get Your Grapefruit Drilled
Milwaukee

If your bowling score suffered at Holler House, you'll feel a lot better about it at Koz's. According to comments in the visitors' book that Duwayne Kosakoski keeps at the bar, his customers are positively thrilled with the totals they rack up in the next room. It seems to help that the game here is miniature bowling. The four alleys are only 16 feet long, the pins are 9 inches high, and the ball is akin to a four-pound grapefruit.

1912. Still, he was removed to Chicago's Mercy Hospital for treatment, even though Mt. Sinai was just down the street.

Teddy was actually shot leaving his hotel on the way to the Milwaukee Auditorium; it was on the ride there that an aide noticed the hole in the president's overcoat. Asking only for a clean handkerchief to stem the blood flow, Roosevelt launched into his stump speech, during which it became clear to his audience that something was dreadfully wrong.

Schrank was eventually confined to the Hospital for the Criminally Insane in Oshkosh. Roosevelt lost his bid for a third term to Woodrow Wilson and suffered lifelong debilities from the wound, complicated by untreated malaria from a subsequent rafting trip in the Amazon (the man obviously did not know from convalescing).

For years Milwaukee suffered image problems due to the assassination attempt. It had nearly recovered when a Milwaukee lad, Arthur Bremer, undid it all by shooting George Wallace in 1972.

At one time mini-bowling was a major pastime in Milwaukee; today Koz's offers the only game in town. "The most honest bowling in America is at Koz's Mini-Bowl," wrote Frank Deford in *Sports Illustrated,* where "almost anybody can bowl a 300. Many folks in the area do their bowling only at Koz's, because the company is good, the beer is cold, and there's hard truth enough in the rest of the world."

Bowling hours are not during school hours, because schoolkids set the pins; not Thursday, because that's league night for eight men's teams; and not when the Packers are playing on television. Travelers

> **Trivia**
>
> Liberace, born Wladziu Valentino Liberace in West Allis, attended West Milwaukee High School, where he almost always won first prize for "Most Original Costume" on Character Day. At various times he was Haile Selassie, Yankee Doodle Dandy, and Greta Garbo. At age fourteen he presented his first piano recital at the Wisconsin College of Music, and at twenty he soloed with the Chicago Symphony Orchestra, under the name Walter Buster Keys.

from all over the world have searched out Koz's Mini-Bowl and Bar and mixed with the neighborhood regulars at 2078 South Seventh Street (at Becher). Call (414) 383-0560 for more information.

Stinks So Good
Monroe

The Chalet Cheese Co-op is the only factory in this country that makes the notoriously funky-smelling limburger. Fifty years ago about one hundred plants made limburger, but tastes change, and now Chalet Cheese stands alone.

Chalet Cheese doesn't offer tours, T-shirts, or tasting parties. It does, however, have a store that sells its products (limburger, brick, and baby Swiss). In an adjoining room you can see the decidedly low-tech, labor-intensive packaging operation: three or four women in white seated at a table wrapping little blocks of limburger in rectangles of parchment paper, then waxed paper, and finally foil. The one million pounds of limburger they wrap annually are sold throughout the United States under various labels; so if you buy domestic limburger, it came from here.

The store is open from 7:00 a.m. to 3:30 p.m. Monday through Friday, 8:00 to 10:00 a.m. Saturday. Chalet Cheese Co-op is located at N4858 Highway N (a roller-coaster-style road) about 4 miles north of Monroe. Call (608) 325-4343 for more information.

Limburger is generally associated with practical jokes and sandwiches, and the best place to appreciate the latter—on buttered toast with a slice of sweet onion and a little honey—is Baumgartner's Tavern in Monroe. Baumgartner's believes there's not a place in the world that sells more limburger sandwiches, and they always serve theirs with a mint. Further reminders of the area's Swiss heritage appear in the form of huge oil paintings of alpine scenes; nearly half a mountain goat, among other hunting trophies; and local guys playing cards—as well as a photo of Miss Limburger in a recent Cheese Days parade.

Baumgartner's Cheese Store and Tavern is on the west side of the Green County Courthouse Square. Hours are 8:00 a.m. to bar time daily. Call (608) 325-6157 for details.

Got Mustard?
Mount Horeb

The night in 1986 that the Boston Red Sox lost the World Series, Wisconsin assistant attorney general Barry Levenson was distraught. Seeking comfort in food, he went to an all-night supermarket and had an epiphany in the condiment aisle: "When I stood before the mustards, a voice spoke to me: 'If you collect us, they will come.'"

The collection began in the basement of his home and moved to a pump house in the backyard. One Saturday morning several years later, with the help of a "Pass the Mustard" human chain, it was moved into a store a few blocks away on Main Street.

Today Barry is curator of the Mount Horeb Mustard Museum and dean of Poupon U, which offers six degrees, at $7.50 per diploma, from Ph.D. (Philosopher of Dijon) to J.D. (Juris Dufus). The museum has more than 4,400 jars of mustard from all over the world, a fine display of antique mustard pots, mustard-in-music items, and many other

The Tourist Troll is one of several trolls from updated Scandinavian folklore along the Trollway of downtown Mount Horeb. Michael J. Feeney is the artist. SKOT WEIDEMANN

things mustard. It sells nearly 500 kinds. The Mustard Piece Theater runs the video *Mustard: The Spice of Nations*.

The Mustard Museum is located at 100 West Main Street in Mount Horeb but is planning to move to Middleton in the fall of 2009. Hours are 10:00 a.m. to 5:00 p.m. daily. It celebrates Mustard Day the first Saturday in August. To check on the move and other mustard news, call (800) 438-6878 or visit www.mustardmuseum.com.

Ja, Das ist Eine Dunce Cap
New Glarus

On May 13, 1845, two valleys' worth of villagers—fewer than 200 people in all—from the Swiss canton of Glarus said farewell to Europe forever and sailed for America. On June 18 they ran out of potatoes; on July 19—by now aboard a riverboat on the Ohio—they were attacked by bloodthirsty mosquitoes. But in Galena, Illinois, they were reunited with the advance guard, two men who had been sent to scout for a place comparable to home and found it in Green County, Wisconsin. Together they walked the last 60 miles.

The soil was rich, water was plentiful, the landscape sort of resembled Switzerland, and the price was right—$1.25 per acre. On July 17, 1845, they purchased 1,280 acres and called their new village New Glarus.

The Swiss Historical Village consists of fourteen buildings that tell the rest of the story. A family of eight lived in the authentic 14-by-16-foot log cabin. In the one-room church, they endured two-hour sermons. The 1880 general store displays standard merchandise as well as examples of what an irrepressible Swiss can do with a sharp knife: intricate memorials carved from beeswax, cathedral-like superstructures of wood, a necklace of fruit pits.

Among other heavy-duty equipment in the blacksmith shop is a *schnitzelbank*, the very one in question in the hearty drinking song that asks *"Ist das nicht eine schnitzelbank? Ja, das ist eine schnitzelbank . . ."* The fully equipped, original one-room *schulhaus* even has a dunce cap—not just some flimsy cone-thing fashioned from a piece of

★ ★

notebook paper, but a sturdy, deadly serious dunce cap. The print shop has all the equipment needed to print the *New Glarus Post* and, among other news clips, Mrs. T. C. Hefty's 20-column-inch recipe for soap: "Dissolve one can Eagle brand lye in one quart of cold rain water . . ."

Further examples of doing things the hard way appear in a building full of farm implements. The ice-harvesting plow implies no rest for the weary farmer, even after he had hung up his corn binder and hay knives for the winter. The village would not, of course, be complete without a cheese factory, of which Green County had 200 a century ago.

Knowledgeable local guides conduct the tours and add interesting asides about their relatives. The Swiss Historical Village, 612 Seventh Avenue, is open daily 10:00 a.m. to 4:00 p.m. May through October. Admission charge. For more information call (608) 527-2317 or go to www.swisshistoricalvillage.org.

The Hills Are Alive with the Sound of Alphorns
New Glarus

New Glarus preserves its Swiss heritage with some unique traditions. For one thing, it has a yodel club, the only one in America, which is responsible for not only much of the yodeling that goes on at its festivals, but also the alphorn blowing and the flag throwing.

The town holds three annual festivals: the Heidi Festival in June, whose highlight is a play presented by local actors (and goats and kittens) about the little Swiss girl with braids and her gruff grandfather; Volksfest, which celebrates Swiss Independence Day on the first Sunday in August at Wilhelm Tell Schützenpark (that's shooting park); and the Wilhelm Tell Festival on Labor Day weekend, with outdoor performances by a large cast of local actors (and goats, cows, and horses) telling the Tell story, in English and German. In addition, all three festivals feature a lot of singing and yodeling and playing of accordions and alphorns. And flag throwing (though nobody remembers what flag throwing is about).

Swiss herdsmen used alphorns to call home before they had cell phones. WISCONSIN DEPARTMENT OF TOURISM

The man who gets credit for the town's first production of Friedrich Schiller's *Wilhelm Tell,* in 1938, is Edwin Barlow. A world traveler with childhood ties to New Glarus and a flair for the dramatic, he returned with visions of staging the drama and building a chalet. The drama has been repeated every year since then, and the chalet is now a museum with an amazing collection from Barlow's travels. Did he shop! Here, for example, are such one-of-a-kind items as Empress Carlotta's jewelry, King Louis XVI's watch, and chips from Pope Innocent III's skull, among three floors of other relics, woodcarvings, scissors cuttings, china, furniture, dolls, and artwork. Once Barlow's home, it is called Chalet of the Golden Fleece and is open by appointment only. Call (800) 527-6838.

Of all this Swissness, one longtime resident observed that New Glarus is more Swiss than Switzerland. For more information go to www.swisstown.com.

Leon Varjian led the Boom Box Parade around the capitol in Madison in 1983 to the tune of "Stars and Stripes Forever," courtesy of community radio station WORT. The fifty band members wore red jackets; the mayor wore a black tuxedo. WISCONSIN DEPARTMENT OF TOURISM

★ ★

Look What I Found with the Dust Bunnies!

Oconomowoc

It's supposed to be good luck to find a cat whisker, so over the years Pauline Bemis got in the habit of picking up a whisker if she happened to see one lying around. She placed each one on a little shelf behind the glass door of a grandfather clock, and now she has a large bundle of cat whiskers, hundreds of them.

The cats that she has owned over the past fifteen years are all represented in the collection: Little Caesar, Figaro, Zachary Robert, Pepper, Mitzie, Tiger, and Blackie. On average a cat probably has twenty-four whiskers, twelve on each side of the nose.

Pauline also has a large rock collection, which was featured at the Oconomowoc Public Library. Just for fun, she included the cat whiskers in the exhibit. Did people ask a lot of questions about the rocks? Not really. They were more curious about the cat whiskers.

Pauline has never counted them and has better things to do than sit around counting cat whiskers. Though semiretired, she teaches music and is active in various music groups. She received Oconomowoc's annual civic award in recognition of her musical involvement and other volunteer efforts.

Return of the Two-Headed Pig

Poynette

The MacKenzie Environmental Center made headlines in May 1999 when the two-headed pig disappeared from its Aliens Museum. The pig was kept in a one-gallon jar filled with formaldehyde, displayed alongside some of nature's other curiosities. (As a sign at the museum entrance gently explains to visiting schoolchildren, occasionally in nature abnormal plants and animals occur.)

"Nothing is sacred," said the sheriff, and announced a $1,000 reward for information through the Crime Stoppers tip line. Two farmers who each happened to have two-bodied, one-headed pigs in jars called to offer them to the museum. "It was real nice of them," said

★ ★

the sheriff. Finally, more than three weeks later, the pig was found on a hiking trail. Sheriff's deputies rushed it to Divine Savior Hospital in Portage to top off the formaldehyde and returned it to the museum. Today the pig is again in the display case that it shares with a four-legged pheasant and a Siamese raccoon.

Other exhibits at the Aliens Museum show a white woodchuck, a white gray squirrel, a white white-tailed deer, a white flathead catfish, a white porcupine (examples of albinism); a black red fox, a black gray squirrel (melanism); and a one-antlered deer skull (hermaphroditism).

MacKenzie Environmental Education Center, W7303 Highway CS, off Highway Q east of Poynette, occupies 280 acres and features wild-life exhibits, museums, and hiking trails. The grounds are open from dawn to dusk year-round except during deer gun season. The wildlife exhibit and museums are open daily 8:00 a.m. to 4:00 p.m. May 1 to mid-October; closed weekends and holidays mid-October through April. Call (608) 635-8110 for more information.

The Chicago Typewriter
Racine

In the middle of the afternoon on November 20, 1933, John Dillinger and five henchmen entered American Trades Bank at Fifth and Main in downtown Racine and told everybody to reach for the sky. An exhibit in the lobby of the Racine Police Station tells what happened after that. Dillinger and his gang took $27,000—and, for their getaway, a police-man's .45-caliber Thompson machine gun and two human shields, the bank president and a bookkeeper.

The exhibit includes the tommy gun, which was recovered later with *John Dillinger* etched into the stock, and elaborates on the gun's role in bootleggers' drive-by shootings and its vivid nickname, the "Chicago Typewriter." It also contains the black shoestrings that the gang used to tie the bank president and the bookkeeper to a tree somewhere in Waukesha County.

Smelt-O-Rama

If you're not from around here, you might find it odd to see grown men in snowmobile suits hanging over a bridge at night, lowering large nets on pulleys and shining flashlights into the water. But after you live here a while, you might not only think nothing of it, you might join them.

It's smelting! (Pronounced with a "sh-" for complete authenticity.) Don't let the fact that they're biting the heads off the live little fish put you off; that merely appeases the smelt gods to ensure a good harvest. The smelt start running to spawn in mid-April (at night, of course; no one likes to be seen spawning) in Lake Michigan and in inland lakes across Wisconsin. You've got to eat the tails, although the heads are optional, according to local custom. They come one way: battered, deep-fried, and washed down with beer, although some folks like to slide 'em down with horseradish, hot sauce, tartar sauce, or, I know, beer. They're delicious, but you've got to eat a lot of them.

Curious? To give them a try, head for downtown Port Washington on the first weekend after Easter. American Legion Post 82 (262-284-4690) typically feeds more than a ton of smelt to some 2,000 or 3,000 aficionados—it's a fund-raiser, so you can feel good about it. Bring your own coolers of beer, and butter and condiments, if needed. The smelt feast takes place at the Legion clubhouse, 435 North Lake Street, across from Veterans Memorial Park.

Whatever you do, remember the tails (or the tail patrol will get you), and don't even think of asking for the batter recipe—it's a secret. But odds are beer helps it cling.

★ ★

Shoestrings? The exhibit says they were donated to the Kenosha County Historical Museum by the bookkeeper, Ursula Patzke.

Apparently Dillinger made the most of his few years on Earth. He stole forty-one chickens from Homer Zook at age twenty, spent nine years in prison for robbing an elderly grocer, and worked his way up to "Public Enemy Number One" before being gunned down at age thirty-one. His WANTED description and set of prints are here, too.

The Racine Police Department is at 730 Center Street (Highway 32) in downtown Racine.

Farewell to the Piano
Roxbury

The Roxbury Tavern has the community feeling of an Irish pub, and from time to time it holds something like an Irish wake. The departed

Trivia

The little town of Roxbury made headlines a few years ago when state archaeologists announced that nearby they had found what may be the oldest pieces of toast in Wisconsin. Scientists tested them, you may be sure, and found that the bread was wheat and at least 125 years old. The toast was found at the site of an old cabin during excavations for the expansion of Highway 12. It was the biggest news in Wisconsin's timeline of toast since 1996, when Mervin Langve of Mount Sterling opened up his late mother's old cookstove and found a piece of toast she must have toasted in about 1950. Mr. Langve has preserved it as a keepsake by mounting the toast on a breadboard and adding some rosemaling for decoration.

is an old piano, one that's at the end of its long life, beyond repair but too beloved to be dumped in the landfill.

The rite of passage begins outdoors with an afternoon of food and beer and live music by a combo. Later on, the piano, until now resting quietly on the sidelines, is stuffed with kindling and newspapers and set on fire. Everyone turns their lawn chairs in that direction and watches as the flames build, the strings go *boing,* and eerie harmonics sound. After about an hour, what's left of the piano collapses to the ground. To comply with local fire regulations, which prohibit fires

It was either this or the landfill.

outdoors except for cooking, a turkey wrapped in foil roasts on top of the piano. The following week, Piano Turkey Soup is on the menu.

The Roxbury Tavern has books, newspapers, and board games instead of a pool table, a jukebox, or a television set. It serves food and drink Tuesday through Sunday and has live music on occasion. If the *n* in the OPEN sign has been moved to the front of the word, come back some other time. The tavern is east of Highway 12 at Highway Y and Kipley Road. Call (608) 643-8434.

The Avis of Groundhogs
Sun Prairie

Jimmy the Groundhog lives on a small farm outside of Sun Prairie in a cement hutch with windows and a bed of hay. Once a year, early in the morning on February 2, a limousine pulls up outside Jimmy's little hutch and transports him into town. Television crews, reporters, city officials, and many others await his arrival. If Jimmy casts a shadow when he emerges from the limo, spring weather is more than six weeks away. The nine generations of Jimmys—like heirs to the throne, they're all related—claim better than 79 percent accuracy. After Jimmy has or has not cast a shadow, he goes on display and you can have your picture taken with him, like Santa Claus.

This Sun Prairie tradition of more than fifty years' standing is followed by breakfast and entertainment. Call (608) 837-4547 for details or visit www.groundhogcentral.com.

Noodled unto Death
Watertown

Some years ago Watertown Goose was an impressive item on the menus of railroad dining cars and elegant restaurants in big cities. But how many fine lady and gentleman diners had a clue about what that goose had been through?

Watertown geese were prized because they had been pampered,

This stuffed overstuffed goose can be seen in the barn behind Octagon House in Watertown, along with pale-red models of livers of a noodled goose (on the right) and a normal goose (left).

hand fed, and overfed until they were hugely overweight, by about twenty pounds. (The geese had correspondingly large livers, which translated into pâté de foie gras.) This was accomplished by force-feeding them specially prepared noodles—big, fat multigrain noodles the size of sausages.

About four weeks before market time, a farmer schooled in the noodled-goose tradition began to make the rounds of his flock, holding each beak open with one hand and dropping the noodles down with the other. Each goose had to be fed several noodles every four or five hours around the clock. This meant that the entire family of

★ ★

a goose-noodler was involved, what with preparing special noodles (guess whose job that was?) and getting up at all hours of the night to noodle the geese.

Geese that got too fat to stand up anymore spent their last days in hammock contraptions. The largest Watertown goose ever shipped weighed 38½ pounds; the average was about 25. In one outstanding year, 150,000 pounds of geese were shipped out of Watertown.

This famous local practice began in the 1880s (PETA didn't exist until 1980) and went on until twentieth-century federal meat-inspection laws forbade commercial butchering in the home—unless, of course, the goose-noodler's family hadn't already discovered that life had more to offer than this.

But the geese that gave their lives for the greater glory of Watertown have not been forgotten. For one thing, the Watertown High School athletic teams are still called the Goslings. For another, thanks to taxidermy, you can see a noodled goose, accompanied by livers (both noodled and normal), in the Plank Road Barn behind Octagon House.

Octagon House, a popular Watertown landmark, is an eight-sided, fifty-seven-room brick house that was completed in 1854 as a family residence. On the grounds is the building where Margarethe Meyer

Trivia

Wisconsin, birthplace of the blow dryer. Two companies that were developing electric blenders—Racine Universal Motor and Hamilton Beach of Two Rivers—were aware that women were using vacuum cleaners to dry their hair. They combined the technologies, and the first successful model was introduced in 1951. It had a nozzle attached to a pink plastic bonnet that fit over the head.

Prairie-Style, Bucket Included

Wingspread, a spectacular Frank Lloyd Wright house of the 1930s, has a fireplace with an opening tall enough for 12-foot logs to stand on end vertically. This innovative design proved impractical because logs burn from the bottom and eventually fall out into the room. Another inventive feature was the disappearing table. At the end of each course, the kitchen staff could pull the table into the kitchen, prepare it for the next course, and slide it back out to the dinner guests.

Innovative furniture was also designed for Wright's S. C. Johnson administration building elsewhere in Racine: three-legged office chairs that promoted good posture. Like some other Wright buildings, at first it had a leaky roof. Wright responded to complaints with "That's how you can tell it's a roof," "That's what happens when you leave a work of art out in the rain," and "Move your chair."

The Johnson Foundation operates Wingspread as a conference facility. It is on Lighthouse Drive in Racine. Public tours are limited to Tuesday through Friday, from 9:30 a.m. to 3:00 p.m. No tours are given during conferences. Check the conference schedule and learn more about Wingspread at www.johnsonfdn.org.

Schurz began the first kindergarten in the United States, in 1856. Its interior depicts a class in session and displays some early teaching tools.

The historic buildings on the property are open to the public daily from May through October. Hours are 10:00 a.m. to 4:00 p.m. Memorial Day through Labor Day, 11:00 a.m. to 3:00 p.m. the rest of the time. Tours begin on the hour. Admission charge. For more information call (920) 261-2796.

★ ★

A Wing and a Prayer
Waukesha

One fine morning in September 1941, flight instructor Dean Crites and his twenty-two-year-old student inspected their two-seater plane and took off from Milwaukee's Curtiss-Wright Airport (today Timmerman Field) for what was to be the student's graduation flight. They had just ascended to 1,000 feet when suddenly there was a loud bang and a big jolt. The tail dropped, and the plane stalled and started in a loop. The student gladly turned the controls over to the instructor, who glided to a safe landing in an alfalfa field.

This naturally formed Wisconsin-shaped rock at the Waukesha County Historical Society and Museum has a pebble precisely at the location of Waukesha. Score one for intelligent design?

Not until they were on the ground did they discover that the entire engine had fallen out of the plane. (It was later pried out of Wisconsin Memorial Park cemetery, where it had been found buried a foot deep.) The very next day the brave lad went up again for his flight test.

A broken propeller blade on display at Waukesha County Airport represents all that is left of the plane today. Other exhibits tell the history of local aviation, from farm fields to jet landing strips. It began in 1912 with eighteen-year-old John Kaminski of Milwaukee, who performed exhibition flights in *Sweetheart,* a Curtiss Pusher biplane that had to be dismantled, shipped by train, and reassembled at the next air show. They also tell more about Dean Crites, who could pick up a handkerchief with the wing tip of his WACO 10, and his brother Dale, pioneer aviators who built their first glider in 1919 and started the local flying school.

Mementos of simpler times include a pocket-size circle of plastic embossed with lines and numbers called a "Time-Speed Distance Computer," a slim pamphlet entitled *How to Fly a Piper Cub,* aviation helmets, and Dale Crites's tan flight suit.

Trivia

The principal product of Van Holten, Inc., of Waterloo is a pickle in a pouch. After dealing in vinegar, pickles, and sauerkraut for forty years, in 1939 the company invented the process of the individually packaged pickle. Today it makes about eighteen million a year. People who need a quick pickle hit buy them at truck stops, movie theaters, convenience stores, concession stands, and prisons. For a total pickle experience, they tip the plastic pouch and drink the brine. You can see historic pictures of people packing pickles and meet the whole Pickle-in-a-Pouch family at www.vanholtenpickles.com.

The exhibits are in the Aviation Museum at Waukesha County Airport/Crites Field, 2525 Aviation Drive. For more information call (262) 521-5249 or visit www.critesfield.com. From exit 294 off I-94, go south on Highway J for 1 mile, then travel west on Northview Road for 0.5 mile, then north on Aviation Drive to the terminal.

A Claim to Fame Previously Overlooked
Waukesha

Dave Kremer is the greatest stacker of bowling balls in the world. His unique skill began at a bowling alley where, just for his own entertainment—because, he says, he is not much of a bowler of bowling balls—he balanced one bowling ball on top of another ball and then a third on

Dave Kremer has to practice in the garage.
COURTESY PERFECT IMPRESSIONS

top of those two. There they stood. An onlooker was impressed. "Do it again and I'll pay you," he said, and became Dave's agent.

After practicing for several years in his garage in Waukesha, Dave earned a place in the bizarre-skills category of the *Guinness Book of World Records*—probably a permanent place, since he seems also to be the world's only bowling-ball stacker. His record is eleven balls. A challenger would need steady hands, good eyes, sturdy toes, a sense of humor, luck, an indulgent mate (if any), and an appreciation for bowling-ball shape (bowling balls aren't perfectly round) and weight distribution.

Dave Kremer has a real job and a family, and he doesn't stack bowling balls every day. But stacking them for fun has led to trips all over the world and to appearances on such TV shows as *Live with Regis and Kathie Lee* (Kathie kissed him on the head) and *Ripley's Believe It or Not!* He was also the December page in Guinness's year 2000 calendar.

Tying the Knot
Wisconsin Dells

After Tara and Scott Joles got married in Las Vegas and returned home to the Dells, they began to think about saving other couples the trip by offering the same experience right here. It seemed like a likely spot— after all, many choose to honeymoon at the Dells.

The Joleses located a building right off the main street (formerly a taxi stand), fixed it up, hauled some pews from an old church, and spiffed up the place with white paint and white satin. They became ordained by the Universal Life Church, a nondenominational Web-based ministry. Since the Dells Bells Wedding Chapel opened four years ago, they've married about 500 couples. Despite the chapel's anything-goes policy, most of them plan traditional-style weddings.

Las Vegas–style wedding packages begin at $295 (use of decorated chapel for thirty minutes, minister's fee, silk bridal bouquet, silk bouton-niere, music) and go up to the $1,500 "We Deserve It All" package (all of the above plus limo, candles, cake, harpist, and more).

★ ★

Isn't it romantic?

One big difference from Vegas is the impulse factor. Wisconsin's five-day waiting period for a license has a chilling effect that prevents couples from dashing next door to the chapel after connecting over a few drinks at the Showboat Saloon. In Vegas the marriage license bureau welcomes couples from 8:00 a.m. to midnight year-round, and the chapels do, too.

Across the street from the wedding chapel is the Museum of Historic Torture Devices. There are probably better choices for the kids. A round of miniature golf, say, also right across the street, would spare them some nightmares and you a lot of questions about the horrible

★ ★

contraptions on view here. Stuff like thumbscrews, the rack, the Chinese death cage, the skull crusher, the heretic's fork, the shrew's fiddle. And please, let's not even talk about Vlad the Impaler. There's no need to embellish in a place like this; the devices are simple (and authentic), and the wall copy explaining each technique is straightforward (some key words are *hideous, ghastly, agonizing, Inquisition,* and *religious*).

The Dells Bells Wedding Chapel is located at 43 La Crosse Street, just past the Wisconsin River and off Broadway. Call (608) 393-4228 or visit www.dellsbellsweddingchapel.com. The Museum of Historic Torture Devices is at 740 Eddy Street. Open mid-May to mid-September. Admission charge. Call (608) 254-2439 or go to www.dellstorture museum.com.

The Good Son

Wisconsin Dells

H. H. Bennett made history when he photographed his son, Ashley, leaping the chasm to Stand Rock in 1886. It was one of the first stop-action photos ever made, thanks to his design for a rubber band–powered shutter, and the photo of Ashley became an icon for the Wisconsin Dells. It also enhanced Bennett's reputation as a landscape photographer, whose stereoscopic views of the Dells were already greatly admired in parlors throughout America.

The nineteenth-century photography studio of the man who helped make the Dells famous has been restored and is open to the public as a Wisconsin Historical Society site. His ingenious tools, hand-operated equipment, glass-plate negatives, and darkroom from another era are all here. You have to wonder what Bennett would think if he poked his head out the door and looked down the street today.

These days a trained German shepherd reenacts Ashley's 5-foot leap over the 47-foot chasm as a highlight of the scenic two-hour Upper Dells boat tour on the peaceful Wisconsin River. (Unlike Ashley, dog and trainer practice with a net.) The trip includes a stroll through Witches Gulch, unique rock formations like Black Hawk's Profile and

Ashley did it on only two legs. DELLS BOAT TOURS

★ ★

Demon's Anvil, Native American lore and legend, and some prehistoric geology. Dells Boat Tours depart several times daily April through mid-November. Take I-90/94 exit 87, then watch for signs as you approach the Wisconsin River bridge. Admission charge. For more information call (608) 254-8555 or visit www.dellsboats.com.

The Bennett museum shop sells not only Bennett prints but also T-shirts bearing his signature photo in tasteful sepia tones and floaty pens with the German shepherd version. H. H. Bennett Studio, 215 Broadway, is open daily May through October, weekends the rest of the year (closed in January). Admission charge. Call (608) 253-3523 or go to www.wisconsinhistory.org/hhbennett.

4

Southwest

Wisconsin's west coast: *Instead of the Pacific Ocean, the Mississippi River. Instead of Malibu or Carmel or San Francisco, think Cassville or La Crosse or Buffalo City. Instead of some thousand-dollar-a-night beach house, try a B&B overlooking the Mississippi. One of them has a National Register of Historic Places sign in front and the following notice inside: "If no one is here, go upstairs and pick a room, keys are in the door. Leave a check [$30] on the dresser. Welcome."*

Inland, the southwest section of Wisconsin is rich in the works of visionary artists—self-taught locals with the urge to say something patriotic, something religious, something personal, something off-the-wall. Years ago they said it with cement, creating massive folk sculptures and smashing the family crockery (that must have been cathartic) for embellishments. Sometimes, a visit to the Dickeyville Grotto was all it took to unleash the artist within. Today, outsider artists are more likely to work in the medium of industrial debris, possibly inspired by the genius of Dr. Evermor's Art Park, south of Baraboo.

In this southwest section of Wisconsin Curiosities *you will not learn how the town of Eleva got its name. According to a popular version of its derivation, the man who was hired to paint the word* ELEVATOR *on a grain elevator quit before painting the last three letters. People coming through the area assumed that Eleva was the name of the town and it stuck. Nitpicky historians, however, disagree, and their less-entertaining versions made it no fun to even bring up the subject.*

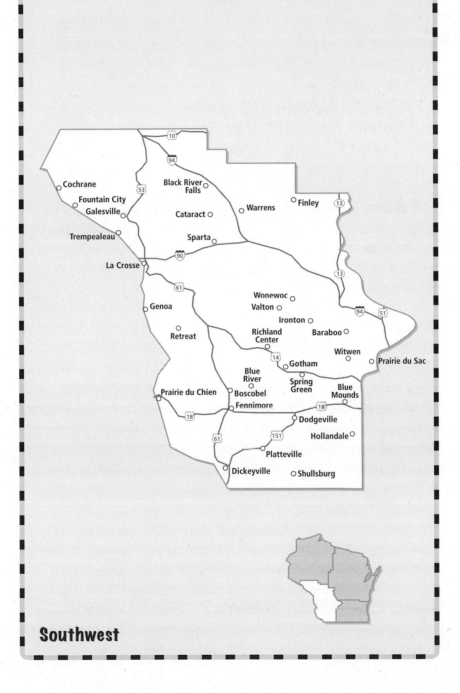

Cochrane

Fountain City
Galesville

Trempealeau

Black River
Falls

Warrens

Finley

Cataract

Sparta

La Crosse

Genoa

Wonewoc
Valton

Ironton

Baraboo

Richland
Center

Witwen

Retreat

Prairie du Sac

Gotham

Blue
River

Spring
Green

Blue
Mounds

Prairie du Chien

Boscobel

Fennimore

Dodgeville

Hollandale

Platteville

Dickeyville

Shullsburg

Southwest

Dr. Evermor's Forevertron,
the world's largest scrap-metal sculpture.

Something Out of Nothing
Baraboo

Several metal creatures alongside the highway and a simple DELANEY'S SURPLUS sign identify Dr. Evermor's location, but they hardly prepare you for what lies behind the trees and down the driveway. It's a fantastic garden of scrap metal, now assembled into giant insectoids and birds; a philharmonic-size bird orchestra; and the 400-ton *Forevertron,* the world's largest scrap-metal sculpture, according to the *Guinness Book of World Records*.

Early in the 1940s, when he was little Tom Every growing up in Brooklyn, Wisconsin, Dr. Evermor was flattening tin cans and toothpaste tubes and saving foil from gum wrappers for the war effort, along with everyone else. With this early conditioning in recycling, he grew up to run an industrial salvage business and to appreciate what industrial designers could do with iron, steel, brass, bronze, and copper. He also developed a fine collection of dynamos, survey markers,

* *

sheet metal, springs, pipes, chains, chimes, wrenches, musical instruments, blades, cables, the decontamination chamber from the Apollo
space mission, and much, much more. With these materials he creates
gigantic yet intricate sculptures.

The *Forevertron* represents Dr. Evermor's plan to travel to the heav-
ens, as a scientist or professor of 1890 might have imagined doing
inside a copper egg propelled by a magnetic lightning-force beam.
Nearly everything else here is centered on the idea—the *Celestial Lis-
tening Ears,* the *Graviton,* the *Juicer Bug,* even the *Bird Band,* which
will be playing as Dr. Evermor sails away. Visiting engineers appreciate
the fact that its components are salvage from late-nineteenth-century
factories.

Dr. Evermor is a self-taught artist who uses no blueprints, no
sketches, nothing. He doesn't even think about it—"I just go for it."
His work attracts television crews, filmmakers, artists, inventors, children, and a great assortment of humanity.

Dr. Evermor's Art Park is on the west side of Highway 12, just north
of Highway C, and 7 miles south of the Baraboo city limits. Consistent
with the creator's spirit, there is no admission fee, no signs to explain
anything. But you might meet Lady Eleanor Every or even Dr. Evermor
on-site, in pith helmet with cigar. For tours call (608) 219-7830.

Flap Your Elbows, Spin Your Ears, and Fly Away
Baraboo

The International Crane Foundation (ICF) has every species of crane in
the world—and George Archibald. He too is a tall and rare bird. "I'd
do almost anything for a crane!" says Archibald, co-founder of the ICF.

Archibald's earliest childhood memory is of being two years old and
crawling after a mother duck and her ducklings. When he got older
his parents let him raise chickens, ducks, pheasants, turkeys, and even
peacocks. By the time he was out of college, he was dancing around
like a crane to encourage female cranes to lay eggs and dressing up
like a crane to take care of young birds.

★ ★

It's all very scientific, as he has explained to audiences far and wide: A newborn crane thinks that the first large moving thing it sees is its mother, so it's important to establish the crane image from the start. Endangered cranes all over the world were in big trouble before Archibald and others at the ICF came to their rescue, and they're all breathing easier now.

The ICF is the only place in the world where you can see all fifteen of the planet's crane species, including the sarus crane, at 6 feet easily the world's tallest flying bird. You might also see some staff "chick parents" dressed like cranes. From chick parents, baby cranes learn where to find food, how to go to water, and to be alert.

The International Crane Foundation is about 5 miles north of Baraboo and 1 mile east of Highway 12 on Shady Lane Road. Hours are

A chick parent at the International Crane Foundation wears a crane costume so that the birds don't get too attached to humans. COURTESY INTERNATIONAL CRANE FOUNDATION

9:00 a.m. to 5:00 p.m. daily, April 15 through October 31. Admission charge. For information about cranes, special events, and tours, see the ICF's Web site at www.savingcranes.org or call (608) 356-9462.

Send in the Clowns
Baraboo

Baraboo is the only place in Wisconsin where elephants splash in the river in summertime. They're taking a break before it's back to work at the Big Top Show at the Circus World Museum.

The performance season runs from mid-May through Labor Day, but you can see exhibits year-round. These could include a splendiferous cornucopia of costumes, from Marcella the elephant's blankets and headpieces (Marcella was with the circus for fifty-five years) to the Queen of Sheba's over-the-top ensemble. Posters tell of intrepid, intricate feats on a single strand of wire at dizzying heights. Also here is the world's largest collection of one-of-a-kind antique circus wagons, huge wood-carved masterpieces that have been painstakingly restored.

It's all here because Baraboo was home until about 1918 to the Ringling Brothers, "The World's Greatest Showmen" (they started out with a small tent, three horses, and a hyena), and to their circus as well.

Located at 550 Water Street (Highway 113). Admission charge. For events, dates, and times, call (866) 693-1500 toll-free or visit www.wisconsinhistory.org/circusworld.

Wisconsin Death Trap
Black River Falls

In an ordinary winter, Black River Falls is an outdoor paradise for snowmobilers, cross-country skiers, dogsledders, and snowboarders. Once it warms, the Black River and the state forest surrounding the handsome little community provide virtually every kind of outdoor experience you could hope for. As the chamber of commerce likes to say, "Nowhere in this great continent of ours can be found a more desirable residence."

★ ★

It's just that, for a few years back in the 1890s, everyone in Black River Falls seemed to go crazy. Michael Lesy captured it in his book *Wisconsin Death Trip* (1973), a pastiche of mortuary photographs, newspaper clippings, and admissions records of the Mendota Mental Asylum culled from the *Badger State Banner*, a tabloid published in Black River Falls by Frank and George Cooper that leaned heavily toward human interest and misery.

For whatever reasons—economic or personal depression, disease, crop failure, just plain loneliness (some have even cited "ethnic tendencies of the Scandinavian and German populations")—all manner of weird goings-on went on. Windows were smashed, children ran wild, fires were set, farmers used dynamite for pillows, and chickens were decapitated in bizarre rituals, all recorded by photographer Charles Van Schaick, whose studios now house the Jackson County Historical Society (where the number-one attraction is his "Wisconsin Death Trip" collection).

It could be that this sort of thing went on in isolated rural areas everywhere in the Midwest, but there was just no Van Schaick to record it. "Wisconsin Death Trip" is now a cottage industry in Black River Falls, and the 1999 film of the same name by James Marsh stirred the pot. The original photos are at the Jackson County Historical Society, 13 South First Street, which is open 10:00 a.m. to 3:00 p.m. Wednesday through Friday or by appointment. Call (715) 284-5314. You can see some of the photographs at www.blackriverfalls.com/area_history.html.

Vroom Vroom
Blue River

Gone are the days when Rod Pasold went roaring around Grant County on his motorcycle. No more the long skids over gravel, the encounters with barbed-wire fences and barns and concrete culverts, the cow stampedes, the emergency rooms. Today Rod leads a quiet life, limping around on land that's been in the family for generations,

Rod's old crutches hang from his Death Row totem pole; motorcycles and helmets march off into the distance.

land set against a backdrop of blue-green hills, wildflowers, and the neighbor's Holsteins.

But wait! Rod's motorcycle days aren't over! They live on at a kind of outdoor museum that displays dozens of bikes and scores of helmets for all to see who pass by on Highway 133. Rod collects them from places like salvage yards and St. Vinnie's resale store in Muscoda. A few are contributions from bikers who pitch their old helmets into the yard as they zoom by. It all looks tempting to the occasional midnight shoppers, as Rod calls them, who may discover in daylight that goods that sit out here year-round are not in such great condition.

As a retired welder with twenty years' experience, Rod is well equipped to get creative with all these materials. His Death Row totem

pole combines a skiff, skis, crutches, and helmets. A motorcycle frame has antlers. Many of the bikes are hybrids, part Suzuki, part Harley, part Honda. Huge kettles that once scalded hogs add a historic note.

It's both motorcycle history and bird sanctuary, where in springtime birds build nests in the helmets and hatch their young.

You can't miss it, on the south side of Highway 133, between Blue River and Muscoda, and Rod welcomes you.

Thou Shalt Not Steal the Toiletries
Boscobel

Janesville salesman John "Nick" Nicholson had had a hard day on the road when he checked into the Boscobel Hotel, or "Central House," as it was known in 1898. He was not pleased (1) to learn that no single rooms were available, and (2) to find the hotel "crowded with drummers and hang-abouts playing cards, shaking dice, smoking, laughing, cursing, yelling and singing with clinking of glasses and men drunk and asleep in chairs." He was, however, willing to share a double room (Room 19) with, as it turned out, a kindred spirit, Beloit salesman Sam Hill.

Nicholson and Hill agreed that "Christian traveling men" needed suitable ways to pass the time, so they organized what eventually became the Gideons International Society. Today the Gideons make sure that hotel rooms all over the world contain Bibles—that's about 59 million Bibles per year, or 112 nightstand drawers per minute.

Senator John F. Kennedy and his wife, Jacqueline, occupied Room 19 for a few hours on the afternoon of March 25, 1960, and then had dinner. JFK was campaigning for the Democratic nomination for president, and the Wisconsin primary was coming up. It is not known how much of that time they spent on Bible study.

The local historical society has outfitted Room 19 in period furniture, and you can ask to see it by calling (608) 375-4714. The 1863 building isn't functioning as a hotel now, but it has a restaurant and bar, as well as a lobby that displays Gideon Bibles in several languages. It is located at 1005 Wisconsin Avenue in downtown Boscobel.

The Wegners embellished their steamship with seashells, plumbing pipes, and drainage pipes. WISCONSIN DEPARTMENT OF TOURISM (R.J. AND LINDA MILLER)

And on the Seventh Day the Wegners Rested

Cataract

Before the era of television and professional football, families piled into their cars and went out for Sunday drives. In this part of Wisconsin, one of the places they headed for, if not over, was Cataract.

The big attraction was the concrete-and-glass creations of Paul and Matilda Wegner. Cars lined up for miles to see the church, the steamship, the anniversary cake, an American flag—thirty sculptures in all. A peace monument even became a "speakers' corner" for preachers and politicians.

The Wegners created all of this during their retirement. They were German immigrants who first farmed and later ran the Ford dealership in the nearby town of Bangor. (They raised five children along the way.) Then one day in 1929, they ventured south to Dickeyville and beheld Father Wernerus's grotto (see page 189). After that experience, sculptures and structures with themes of patriotism, religion, and travel

began taking shape on their own property.

The Wegners used pieces of glass and pottery, many a blue transformer, here and there a doorknob, and, of course, concrete. The profusely embellished exterior of the glass church has views of eleven different churches; the interior is equally intricate. It was the scene of many weddings as well as Paul Wegner's funeral. The steamship represents the Wegners' voyage to this country in 1886, and the giant wedding cake honors their fifty-two years together.

The Kohler Foundation funded restoration of the site and deeded the Paul and Matilda Wegner Grotto to Monroe County, which maintains it as an outdoor museum and public park. Located 9.2 miles north of Sparta off Highway 27, west on Highway 71 near the town of Cataract. Open Memorial Day through Labor Day. For more information call the Monroe County Local History Room at (608) 269-8680 or visit www.monroecountyhistory.org/wegnergrotto.php.

One Cure for Old-Age Boredom

Cochrane

Herman Rusch was another energetic, self-taught, late-blooming artist who emerged in the 1950s. At age seventy-one he discovered his medium to be glass and cement. He proceeded to spread his whimsical dinosaurs, flamingos, polar bears, snakes, and a Hindu temple over several acres of land south of Cochrane, near the Mississippi River. He also surrounded them with ornamental spires and gates and enclosed them in a spectacular, 260-foot-long arching fence. "You could go around the world five times and never see another like it," he said.

Rusch's work has won high praise for its sense of design and wit, but Herman seemed not to have taken himself too seriously. According to the inscription on a bust of himself, creating this wondrous world was just "a good way to kill old-age boredom." He died in 1985, eleven days after his one-hundredth birthday, having successfully lived up to his claim that "a fellow should leave a few tracks."

Herman's "tracks" were restored by the Kohler Foundation, which

Herman Rusch's signature piece. WISCONSIN DEPARTMENT OF TOURISM

also assisted with the addition of a new exhibit, a collection of eighteen miniature buildings modeled after actual buildings in Cochrane. About 2 feet tall, they were created in the Depression era by yet another self-taught artist, Fred Schlosstein, in his backyard on Main Street and now stand in the Prairie Moon museum. Some Schlosstein sculptures are being added outside.

To reach the Prairie Moon Sculpture Garden and Museum, take Highway 35 northwest from Fountain City about 6 miles. Just past the Cochrane–Fountain City School, turn left onto Prairie Moon Road; the site is located a half mile farther, on the left. The garden is open year-round, dawn to dusk. The museum is open by appointment or by chance. Call (608) 687-8250 for more information.

Hazards off the bike trail: at the corner of Highway M and Fitchburg Road south of Fitchburg (left) and between Highway ID and South Street in Blue Mounds (below).

ERICA SCHLUETER (TOP);
JERRY MINNICH (BOTTOM)

Holy Ghost Park
Dickeyville

In both mass and message, the Dickeyville Grotto is the weightiest of Wisconsin's cement parks. No whimsical creatures cavort here. Instead there are awesome altars and shrines labeled with straightforward commands—faith, peace, chastity, mildness, long suffering, patience, fortitude—and encrusted with glassware, pottery, fossils, Indian relics, and hornets' nests.

This is the work of Father Mathias Wernerus, who, in the 1920s, saw it as "God's wonderful material collected from all parts of the world. . . Future generations will still enjoy the fruit of our labor and will bless the man that conceived and built this thing." He was right. Each year about 60,000 people view the altars, shrines, fountains, gardens, and sculptures on the grounds of Holy Ghost Parish.

Father Wernerus, a missionary priest who grew up among outdoor shrines in Germany, had a lot of assistance from parishioners

One of the "Religion in Stone" areas at Holy Ghost Park at Dickeyville. WISCONSIN DEPARTMENT OF TOURISM

189

★ ★

and schoolchildren. They hauled rocks and concrete, contributed materials from home, and helped with decoration and construction. The Dickeyville Grotto is actually a collaborative project representing the geology of the upper Mississippi region, the religious and patriotic beliefs of Father Wernerus and his parishioners, and the crockery and figurines of their combined households.

The grotto is on Highway 61 just west of Highway 151. Grounds open year-round; tours daily in summer months. Call (608) 568-3119 for details.

Is That a Stratocruiser, or Are You Just Happy to See Me?
Dodgeville

A few miles south of House on the Rock (see page 219), while your head is still spinning, you come upon a Boeing C-97 Stratocruiser parked alongside Highway 23. It's the size of half a football field, and during the Korean War it transported troops and cargo.

It's a landmark for the Don Q Inn, which lies just beyond. The elaborate plans that Don Quinn, who owned the hotel then, had in mind for the plane didn't quite work out, but other ideas have. The Dodgeville train station was moved here and converted to sleeping rooms, the steeple from an 1850s Methodist church became a honeymoon suite, copper cheese vats were converted to bathtubs, and barber chairs from shops in Fennimore and an Iowa penitentiary offer seating in the lobby.

It isn't exactly the plane and local history that bring many people here, however. The Don Q has fantasy suites that offer travelers an opportunity to bed down in a space capsule, a thatched jungle hut, Caesar's court, or a hot-air balloon, among other novel accommodations.

All this is connected to the Don Q restaurant by a damp, 300-foot-long stone tunnel. Located on Highway 23 North. Call (608) 935-2321 for information or visit www.donqinn.net.

The Whad'Ya Gnome hopes to meet a cute little girl gnome at the Don Q tonight. JERRY MINNICH

When Eric Wallner started to build on his rural property north of Dodgeville, this is the first building he completed. With praying-hands motif, double doors with brass piano hinges, and parquet floor, it may be the only Prairie-style outhouse in the country. It also has a panoramic view of the countryside. Eric's new home (with indoor plumbing) is just a few miles from Taliesin, Frank Lloyd Wright's home and studio. He is an architect and has worked on Wright restorations.

Cogito, Ergo Zoom
Finley

Did a few of the Cub Scouts seem bored on the tour of the cranberry bog? Were they dragging their feet on the nature trail? If so, here's a field trip that could be a winner: bombing practice at the Hardwood Range.

Here crews from Truax Field in Madison and other Midwest bases of the Air National Guard are training in their F-16s, F-15Es, and other incredibly fast planes. The bombs are inert, shadows of their former shells; no actual bombs are harmed in the preparation of these crews for combat. The targets vary: an old beat-up SCUD missile launcher, little bridges, fuel storage tanks, big orange bull's-eyes, jeeps, a rusty PT boat.

This 12-foot fiberglass mouse is named for the great Russian composer Igor Stravinsky, who died on the day that Igor arrived in Fennimore, April 6, 1971. He stands in front of Fennimore Cheese on Highway 61 on the south side of Fennimore.
COURTESY FENNIMORE CHEESE

★ ★

The range is more than 2 miles wide by 6 miles long, which is plenty of room for an F-16 to come screaming across the sky. You have to supply your own KABLAAAMs and BARROOOOOOMs, however, because the bombs don't make a sound—they just kick up a big gray cloud on the ground. The surrounding area is heavily wooded and probably devoid of forest creatures, who may have fled to the Necedah Wildlife Refuge on the other side of Highway 80. Flights are restricted there.

The public is welcome. Picnic tables, a Pepsi machine, a restroom, airplane posters for your bedroom wall, and earplugs are provided. Located about 12 miles north of Necedah. Call (608) 427-1509 for a recorded message of the daily schedule, driving directions, and news of upcoming events. Read more about it at www.volkfield.ang.af.mil/index.html.

A lot of people like cranberry bogs, but they're not for everyone.

House on the Rock? No, Rock in the House
Fountain City

At 11:38 a.m. on April 24, 1995, Maxine Anderson was admiring her newly decorated bedroom—the wallpaper with its tiny blue flowers and border of cabbage roses, the full-length mirrors on the closet doors—when she heard a noise that was worse than thunder. She headed for the door, and seconds later a fifty-five-ton boulder landed where she had been standing. For thousands of years it had hovered high up on the bluff behind the house. (Today you can look up and see the gap, like a missing tooth, in a row of boulders like this one.) The Andersons promptly moved out and sold the house as is, rock, debris, and all, to people with an eye for its tourism possibilities.

Strangely enough, the same thing happened to a house next door in April 1901. This runaway rock, however, killed a Mrs. Dubler as she slept. Her husband awoke to find himself in the cellar amid the ruins of their home. A garage stands on the site now. Stranger still, yet another boulder—enormous, 200 tons—careened down the bluff in 2002, but only trees were in the way of that one.

This is not the look the Andersons had in mind for the master bedroom. WISCONSIN DEPARTMENT OF TOURISM

Fountain City has antiques stores, art galleries, and a fatalistic population. Rock in the House is located toward the north end of town and faces the Mississippi River, at 440 North Shore Drive (Highway 35, the Great River Road). Open—is it ever—daily from 10:00 a.m. to 6:00 p.m., year-round. Call (608) 687-6106 for more information.

★ ★

The Joys of Toys

Fountain City

Elmer Duellman owned forty cars by the time he was eighteen years old. It was a sign of things to come. Now in his fifties (and driving a red Nissan pickup truck), he shows what he's collected since then at Elmer's Auto and Toy Museum. Actually, Elmer likes anything with wheels. In addition to cars for grown-ups, he has more than 600 pedal cars—the Junior G-man cruiser with tommy gun mounted on the fender is especially eye-catching—and more than 100 pedal tractors. He even has a bookmobile.

Elmer's wheels and toys are housed in five positively jam-packed barnlike buildings. In one you can see everything from a two-tone green 1933 Rolls-Royce and a silver Corvette with 4.5 miles on the odometer to a Gene Autry bike with fringed saddlebags bearing the Autry-twirling-his-lariat motif. Elsewhere behold an orange and black 1975 Excalibur Phaeton, a 1968 Chevrolet Caprice, and a 1929 Model A Ford Phaeton, this last in the family room—Elmer is lucky that his wife, Bernadette, shares his enthusiasm. Altogether they have more than a hundred cars, plus great numbers of motorcycles, scooters, riding toys, and antique toys and dolls.

To top it off, Elmer's Auto and Toy Museum has a spectacular location on Eagle's Bluff, the highest point on the Mississippi River, with a panoramic view of the main channel and backwaters. To get there, take Highway 95 for half a mile from Fountain City to Highway G, then go a quarter mile to W903 Elmers Road. Admission charge. The hours are tricky—something like every other weekend in summer—so before you go, call (608) 687-7221 or check out the schedule at www .elmerautoandtoymuseum.com.

★ ★

Serendipity in Hardware

Genoa

The words "Ohmigosh, I've been looking for this for years" ring out at Old Tool Shed Antiques. Gayhart Swenson and his son Rick lovingly rescue, clean, repair, display, and sell old hand tools. Handmade tools are especially admired here, from the simple plumb bobs that boys made in high school shop class to very complex contraptions. In addition to hundreds of hammers, chisels, and drills are the more offbeat fire-hose nozzles (Gay and Rick are both retired firefighters), rope winders, ornate cast-iron tractor seats, goose-wing axes, denture makers, cigar-box openers, and much more that you'll never see at Home Depot.

Some items at Old Tool Shed Antiques are so old that hardly anyone knows what they ever were used for. Hardly anyone, because it's really a matter of waiting for the right person to come through the door. Not long ago a mystery tool sat on the front counter for several months until at last a stranger entered the shop and with one glance announced, "I know what that is, and I have the instruction booklet at home." On his next visit, instructions and Mend-a-Rip (a hand-sewing device that cowboys carried to repair saddles and chaps) were reunited.

You might want to celebrate finding that wrench that completes your set over a platter of catfish cheeks at one of the local restaurants. Genoa (pronounced "GeNOa," despite its Italian heritage) is on the Mississippi River, 17 miles south of La Crosse on Highway 35 (the Great River Road). Old Tool Shed Antiques occupies an 1867 building at 612 Main Street. Open 10:00 a.m. to 4:30 or 5:00 p.m. Thursday through Monday, or by chance or appointment. Call (608) 689-2066.

Eat Your Heart Out, Claes Oldenburg

Gotham

In February 1999 a winter ice storm damaged a tall conifer in a small grove of Norwegian spruces at the Merry Farm of Gotham. When the broken branches were cleared away, the owners saw that the forces of

The historical felt-tip marker at Merry Farm of Gotham.
Sculpture by Michael Feeney. KERRI MARSHALL-EDGERLY PHOTOS

★ ★

Nature had selected their property as the site of a modern icon: a felt-tip marker, 9 feet tall. They commissioned a wood sculptor to smooth out the contours and added a bronze plaque declaring it a historical marker.

The marker stands between a brown house and a brown barn in a small grove of tall pine trees. The owners are friendly. The property has beautiful gardens and has been the scene of weddings, workshops, and celebrations of all kinds. (One bride, somewhat peeved because her husband invited his horses to join the wedding party at the last minute, instead of saying "I will" said, "If you change your attitude, I will.")

Take Highway 14 to Gotham; go east on Highway JJ for three-quarters of a mile and north on Moss Hollow for 1 mile; at the sharp turn right, go straight to the end of Slow Lane to number 30999.

Art for Nick's Sake

Hollandale

Nicholas Engelbert was different from other dairy farmers. He read a book while walking his cows along the highway to graze (he owned only fourteen acres). And on the lawn of his farmhouse were all these creations that he put together when he got home: Paul Bunyan, Uncle Sam, Snow White and the Seven Dwarfs, Vikings, lions, elephants, eagles, peacocks. He used metal parts from around the barnyard, stones from the stream, glass and china from the kitchen, and concrete for glue. As if Nick had a lot of glass-and-concrete batter left over one day, the exterior of his two-story house acquired a facade to match the sculptures.

The Engelbert place eventually became quite a roadside attraction, so Nick provided a parking lot and picnic grounds for visitors. Every year his wife planted flowers that spelled out PEACE.

But Nick died on his eighty-first birthday in 1962, and his artwork fell into disrepair. Pieces disappeared, though the mailman tried to keep an eye on things. In 1991 the Kohler Foundation came to the rescue. It restored many pieces, gave Nick's place a name—Grandview—and turned the project over to the Pecatonica Foundation, which operates Grandview as a historic folk-art site. The house is now a museum, and Nick's paintings of family life hang on the walls.

Grandview is located on the south side of Highway 39 just west of Hollandale. The museum is open 10:00 a.m. to 4:00 p.m. Tuesday through Sunday from Memorial Day through Labor Day; the grounds are open daily year-round. Call (608) 967-2322 or (608) 967-2122 or visit www.nicksgrandview.com for more information.

Nick Engelbert depicted his family in this family tree. He and his wife are on the lower branches, their children are playing and doing hobbies they liked, and the fellow at the bottom is one of the tramps who enjoyed the Engelberts' hospitality over the years.

For years Lester Fry collected the turquoise and clear glass insulators that used to serve on power poles, and he created trees like these that he then planted in his front yard. Insulators arch over the front steps to the house. Another arrangement incorporates the dinner bell from the dairy farm where he grew up. Morning glories engulf them in the backyard in summer. Lester Fry died in 1996, but his work still festoons the yard of his longtime home in Ironton (pop. 660) at 571 Mill Street (Highway 58).

★ ★

The world's largest six-pack is 54 feet high and holds 68,200 gallons of beer (enough to fill 1,223,466 normal six-packs) during the aging process. It is located at City Brewery just south of downtown La Crosse. Heading south on Rose Street (Highway 53), go 5 blocks past the blue bridge (Cass Street) and under the overpass to the six-pack and the City Brewery hospitality center. COURTESY CITY BREWERY

They Call Him Google Man

La Crosse

Do you remember who spilled Kool-Aid in the backseat on the way to Lake Sissabaggama on July 17, 1968? Or the picture on the postcard you mailed to Grandma?

What was under the Christmas tree in 1989? The name of that movie you saw last week? Neither do I, but Brad Williams of La Crosse remembers the details of almost every day of his life, after the age of four or five.

He also knows what was happening elsewhere—just ask him. Who sang "The Star-Spangled Banner" before Super Bowl XXV? When did Mt. St. Helens erupt? What celebrity marriage took place on October 6, 1991? What well-known person died on October 14, 1977?

Brad doesn't know what he never knew, of course (for instance, words beginning with *kh,* when he was on *Jeopardy!*), but he does know what he ever knew, with an amazing combination of recall and cross-referencing.

His family was so used to Brad's coming up with all kinds of details about everything that nobody gave it a second thought. But just a couple of years ago Brad's brother Eric read about a woman in California with the same kind of autobiographical memory. Eric got in touch with the scientists who were studying her, and before long they were scanning Brad's brain, too. That made only two of them—possibly a third in Ohio—with the condition called hyperthymesia, "an extraordinary capacity to recall specific events from their personal past." Eric, a screenwriter, is working on a documentary about Brad entitled *Unforgettable*.

Brad is a broadcaster at news-talk radio station WIZM in La Crosse, is really good at Scrabble, and isn't married, which is just as well since it's said that the secret to a happy marriage is a short memory. He has been the official pronouncer for the state spelling bee since 1978 (as an eighth-grader he represented Wisconsin at the national bee).

Just so he doesn't show up to play the *Whad'Ya Know* quiz, or there goes the whole kielbasa.

M as in Mickey

Platteville

The 241-foot letter *M* that overlooks Grant County from a mound east of Platteville is the work of energetic and competitive students of the Wisconsin Mining School in the late 1930s. Other mining schools had big *M*s, but the Wisconsin boys made sure that they hauled enough limestone to make their school's the biggest.

More than 260 steps lead to the top of the big M, but once there you'd have to be about 20 feet tall to view the world's largest W. You can, however, survey the countryside for miles around or zoom in on tiny cows with the telescope provided here. WISCONSIN DEPARTMENT OF TOURISM

The *M* is lighted at night on two annual occasions: University of Wisconsin–Platteville homecoming in the fall, and the "M" Ball in the spring. Members of a coed professional engineering fraternity accomplish this by placing about 500 coffee cans around the outside of the *M*. Inside each can is a smaller can, with a few rocks between the two for ballast. Kerosene and a particle-board wick go into each smaller can. Theta Taus dash around with road flares lighting the wicks, and the *M* burns for about forty-five minutes.

In 1998 a member of the Platteville Jaycees had a brilliant idea. He rounded up about 250 Plattevillians who were willing to dress in black (black trash bags, if necessary), trudge up the 260 steps, and arrange themselves in the shape of mouse ears in the V part of the *M*. An aerial photographer snapped the scene, and the photo won for Platteville the grand prize in a nationwide contest sponsored by Disney: Mickey's Hometown Parade. On July Fourth about 50,000 people (many in mouse ears) lined Main Street to see such sights as thirty Disney floats; the Cuba City High School band in Pluto hats; and Mickey, Minnie, and Donald, waving and bowing. That night $100,000 worth of fireworks went off at the world's biggest *M*.

The *M* is about 4 miles northeast of Platteville on Highway B, but it's best viewed from miles away. Students from the College of Engineering, Mathematics and Science maintain the *M*. For a complete history, beginning with the first *M* created in 2 feet of snow in 1936 by two local lads, go to www.platteville.com/attract.htm#m.

The Beaumont Diet
Prairie du Chien

The exhibits on early medicine at the Prairie du Chien Museum at Fort Crawford are positively chilling—especially "Doctors on Horseback" from the 1840s. You'd have to be in pretty bad shape to be glad to see one of these guys coming up the driveway. In his saddlebags might be a pocket surgical kit of handmade instruments, a lancet or "scarificator" for bleeding, a turnkey for extracting teeth. But the price was right: In 1846 the bill for one patient came to only $46, including $10 for "amputating all the toes of one foot." Doc's snowshoes and lantern complete the picture in this exhibit.

Things improved slightly later on. There were dentists with offices (and foot-operated drills) and horse-and-buggy doctors with manufactured, though still scary-looking, instruments that came in nice lined cases.

A diorama at the Fort Crawford medical museum depicts an amputation on a patient who appears to have passed out. Anesthesia didn't come along until 1846. Medicine was more casual then—doctors in street clothes, leg in bucket, surgical saw on floor.

It was at Fort Crawford that Dr. William Beaumont conducted experiments on the hapless Alexis St. Martin, a voyageur who had suffered a gunshot wound to his left side that left a hole after it healed. Dr. Beaumont found it fascinating to tie bits of food to a string, drop them into the hole, then pull them out to see the effect of Alexis's stomach juices. This went on for several years of codependence, after which, in 1833, Dr. Beaumont published the book that explained the physiology of digestion once and for all. His work is recognized here, along with other milestones in medicine. Dioramas show foot-tall medical professionals calmly removing tumors and amputating limbs, the patients' little faces contorted in agony, until, at last, *anesthesia!* in 1846.

The Prairie du Chien Museum at Fort Crawford, 717 South Beaumont Road, is open daily from 10:00 a.m. to 5:00 p.m. May through October. Admission charge. Call (608) 326-6960 for more information.

A Fish Called Lucky

Prairie du Chien

It's 11:59 p.m. on New Year's Eve. In Times Square, a dazzling Waterford Crystal ball with state-of-the-art lighting effects begins to descend. Several hundred thousand people cheer, and about a billion people worldwide join TV host Dick Clark in the countdown to the new year. In downtown Atlanta, an 800-pound fiberglass peach is lowered from a fancy tower. Thousands kiss and scream as spectacular fireworks light up the sky.

And in Prairie du Chien, a forty-pound carp is slowly lowered from a crane as hundreds—maybe a thousand—people wave sparklers and sing "Auld Lang Syne" and "God Bless America."

It's the Droppin' of the Carp, an annual celebration that Tom and Cathie Nelson dreamed up on their way home from Atlanta, where they'd seen that giant peach: We could do something like that in Prairie du Chien . . . but what would we drop?

Let's see. Prairie du Chien, Mississippi River, fishing—the Nelsons own Willy and Nellie's, a combination boat rental/bike rental/bait shop/root beer stand/minigolf course—of course, carp!

Plans fell into place, and now it's an annual event. Sometime in the fall, the Nelsons' friend Mike Valley stashes a big carp in his freezer at Valley Fish and Cheese. A few days before New Year's Eve, Mike takes out the carp, hereafter known as Lucky, and grooms it, maybe curling the lips. After all, everybody will be lining up after midnight to kiss it for good luck in the new year. A guy from Iowa brings his crane every year for the hoist.

By now, Droppin' of the Carp has expanded to include a tag football game between the fire departments of Prairie du Chien and the Mar-Mac Fire Department across the river. There's also a giant carp piñata for the kids and the crowning of the Carp King and Queen, who later on will be in the St. Patrick's Day Parade.

After all the festivities, Lucky goes back in Mike's freezer until the first Sunday in May, when the fish is buried in what by now has become Lucky Park, and a tree is planted over the grave.

The annual Droppin' of the Carp takes place on St. Feriole Island near the Mississippi River. For details, check with the Nelsons at (608) 326-8602. To be considered for the title of king or queen, apply to Royalty Committee, 128 South Prairie Street, Prairie du Chien, WI 53821. Recently a plasma physicist and an assistant district attorney reigned.

Chips Happen
Prairie du Sac

To the officials of the Wisconsin State Cow Chip Throw, the competitive tossing of dried cow manure is a serious matter: Contestants must select their chips from the wagonload provided by the Official Meadow Muffin Committee. Only two chips per contestant. Chips shall be at least 6 inches in diameter. No gloves. After all, a trip to the national championship in Beaver, Oklahoma, is at stake.

Ammunition for the Cow Chip Throw is collected from cow pastures by community-spirited volunteers, then sun-dried. Other annual events include the Tournament of Chips Parade, 5K and 10K runs, jugglers and magicians, arts and crafts, music and dancing, food and beer.

The event is held on Labor Day weekend. Follow the signs off business Highway 12 (Water Street) to Marion Park. Call (608) 643-4317 to inquire and register to throw. For more information see www .wiscowchip.com.

In Wisconsin We Say, "Forward!"
Retreat

A two-way parade—one that proceeds to the end of the parade route, turns around, and comes back—is extremely rare, but it's a regular feature of the World's Fair in the rural community of Retreat. Not only does the parade last longer that way, but you get to see both sides of the floats and the horses.

The parade starts at the old cheese factory and doubles back at Ames Feed Store, which is the extent of Retreat, or about half a mile.

Kay Hankins of Prairie du Sac, an eight-time Cow Chip champion and a ten-time winner of the World Cow Chip Throw in Beaver, Oklahoma. Her overhand baseball throw and preference for heavier chips contributed to her long reign. JAN MANGIN

★ ★

Retreat's population is small—too small to register on the census taker's radar—so neighbors like De Soto, a Mississippi River village just over the ridge, join in the grand procession. There are old and new farm machines, rescue vehicles, trucks of local businesses like a veterinarian and a septic system service, and original floats by school and church groups. A convertible full of Vernon County royalty passes by, along with the De Soto High School marching band in maroon and gold. Gary Gilbertson provides live coverage for listeners tuned in to Viroqua's radio station WVRQ (1360 AM): "It's an amazing, amazing parade here at the Retreat World's Fair!"

At a pace of about 8 mph and with an intermission while the whole thing gets turned around (Retreat doesn't have any side streets—two-lane Highway N is it), the parade lasts about an hour. Afterward everyone lines up outside the food tent, where lunch and hundreds of homemade pies await. Local talent presents a program on the wooden stage of the 1928 community building, and a horse show goes on all day. That night a dance ends the fair. People from all over come to the Retreat World's Fair, an annual event since 1919.

Retreat is on Highway N in the southwest corner of beautiful Vernon County, and the fair is held on a Saturday in late September or early October. Find out when at www.visitvernoncounty.com.

West Wing West
Richland Center

The approach to Richland Center from the east would be the usual landscape of Kwik Trips and Dairy Queens except for the startling sight of—what's this looming on the horizon?—a huge white dome and a gigantic American flag waving in the breeze. Perkins? No. Our nation's Capitol? No, it's the White House Supper Club and its hospitality partner, the Ramada Inn. With portico, columns, and dome, it's a hybrid one-story rendition of two Washington buildings we know so well.

Welcome to the White House.

★ ★

Step right in (no security searches) and behold the translucent rotunda, the columns, the oil portraits of presidents in the Victorian sitting room, the reservations desk, the coin-operated toy dispenser.

In some kind of corporate shuffle of things, the roles seem to have been reversed. Now that the restaurant is a Country Kitchen done up in country kitsch, it's been left to Ramada to carry out the theme of the original concept. It has done so, down to the winding staircase past more presidential portraits to the Oval Room with its marble pillars and period chandelier, the bar, the meeting rooms named for Washington, Lincoln, Kennedy, and Roosevelt. There's even a display case of thirty-six little lead presidents to scale—LBJ is the tallest and also the last. Whoever started this drew the line at Nixon.

Guest rooms have state names as well as numbers—room 103 is North Dakota, 107 is Illinois, 110 is Colorado, and so on. Rooms have microwaves, VCRs, hair dryers, leather recliners—more than you can say for that Lincoln Bedroom out east. Look for the big white dome of the Ramada Inn and White House Supper Club just off Highway 14 at 1450 Veterans Drive. Call (608) 647-8869 or go to www.whitehouse lodge.com.

To top off the experience, on your way out of town, behold the sight of 300 large U.S. flags on tall poles, representing area servicemen and women. It's a project of the American Legion, on Highway 14 on the west side of Richland Center. If it's a windy day, lower the car window and take in the eerie sound produced by 300 flags all aflutter.

You could even extend your salute to America by traveling on to the Little Falls Railroad and Doll Museum to see all of the First Ladies, from Martha to Michelle, in their inaugural gowns, as portrayed by 16-inch Madame Alexander dolls. Try picturing them paired up with their little lead partners back in Richland Center. The museum is near Cataract, 9208 Highway II. Open 1:00 to 5:00 p.m. Thursday through Monday, April 1 to October 31. Admission charge. For more information call (608) 272-3266 or visit www.raildoll.org.

Miner Transgressions

Highway U in Shullsburg is also known as Judgement Street. That and other street names (such as Truth, Peace, Charity, Faith, and Friendship) reflect the influence of Father Samuel Mazzuchelli, who, back in the 1800s, thought that it wouldn't hurt to remind the rowdy miners of this area of a few biblical virtues.

For insight into the miners' lives, you can visit an 1827 hand-dug lead mine and experience the small spaces and rugged working conditions. No wonder they acted out after a twelve-hour day down there. The Badger Mine and Museum are at the village park on West Estey Street, open daily from 10:00 a.m. to 4:00 p.m., Memorial Day through Labor Day. Call (608) 965-4860 for more information.

Law of Gravity Repealed
Shullsburg

A short length of pavement on Highway U south of Shullsburg is known far and wide as Gravity Hill. Farmers are used to seeing folks from all over creation out here on this little two-lane road, bean fields on both sides, lurching around as they stop their cars, back up, turn around, and try it again. The big attraction is the eerie sensation that occurs when your eyes say you're going downhill but your car says you're going uphill.

To try it, start from the Shullsburg water tower. Your destination is only about 1 mile south. After you pass Rennick Road on your left (at about 0.8 mile) and are heading downhill, look for a yellow, diamond-shaped sign with a black arrow and a 25 mph sign below. About three-fourths of the way to the bottom of this hill but before you get to the sign, stop, put the car in neutral, and feel it roll—uphill.

★ ★

For the thrill of Gravity Hill, stop right here and shift into neutral.

If you like optical illusions (if that's what it is), here are two more. In Madison, from the top of O'Sheridan Street, keep your eye on the capitol across Monona Bay and watch it get smaller—appear to shrink away—instead of larger as you approach it. (O'Sheridan is the first right off Lakeside Street from John Nolen Drive.) At Maiden Rock, across Lake Pepin, is Point–No Point, which appears to "melt away and fold back into the bank," as Mark Twain described it. It helps to be on the Mississippi River to appreciate this one.

★ ★

Or Instead of Fruitcakes . . .

Sparta

The call for illuminated manuscripts had tapered off a lot over the past millennium, so a few years ago the monks of the Cistercian Abbey near Sparta updated the tradition. Operating under the name Laser-Monks, they began to sell printing and imaging supplies for computers at big discounts.

The idea came to Father Bernard McCoy when he was shopping for inkjet printer cartridges. Twenty-five or thirty dollars struck him as sinfully high for a small amount of black powder. It was the Barbie principle: Your first Barbie is not a big investment, but it doesn't end there. It's everything you need to keep her going that runs into big money—Barbie's cheerleader outfits, her convertible, her beach house, her musical dream castle. Barbie is high-maintenance, and so are computers and copiers. Monks, on the other hand, are low-maintenance—"We do monk things," says Father Bernard. Prayer, study, and Gregorian chants occupy much of the day at the Cistercian Abbey's picturesque rural setting (Barbie could take a lesson). The overhead is low, and that's the secret of LaserMonks' success.

Through arrangements with several large companies that make compatible and remanufactured products, LaserMonks, as an outsourcer, began to sell toner cartridges, inkjet cartridges, and copier toner at low prices, with satisfaction guaranteed and divine customer service. The monks (there are only six of them) weren't out to make a huge profit for themselves—they just wanted to meet the expenses of the abbey and support some charities. But sales of $2,000 in 2002 have grown into the millions, and the list of charities now includes food pantries, children's camps, literacy programs, and other helpful works around the world.

The idea of LaserMonks was to offer nonprofits an alternative to the high prices charged by the original equipment manufacturers (just as Barbie might get a better deal if she shopped somewhere besides

★ ★

Mattel). That worked out well and now LaserMonks also offers other kinds of office and school supplies and some food items. You can read about them at www.lasermonks.com.

Where Giant Sombreros Come From
Sparta

Remember the huge hot pink frog with the slippery yellow tongue that you slid down about fifteen water parks ago? It came from the folks at FAST (Fiberglass Animals, Shapes, and Trademarks) in Sparta. So did the pelican slide and the Octoswing. Did you get a drink from the jaws of a hippo fountain, or gas up at the Sinclair station with the 40-foot dinosaur at the Dells? They came from here, too.

FAST specializes in gigantic theme-park creatures, landmarks, and trademarks, and it probably made your favorite, whether it's the

FAST, home of all creatures great and gargantuan. ANDY KRAUSHAAR

216

50-foot Jolly Green Giant in Blue Earth, Minnesota; the world's largest killer bee in Hidalgo, Texas; or the 200-foot sombrero in South Carolina—not to mention many of those chickens and clowns at fast-food places. Even abroad you can't miss their work: the 26-foot pirate in Japan, the elk in Beirut, or the gorilla on a hillside in Colombia, where you can stand in its chest and survey the water park below through a telescope. Furthermore, since fiberglass lasts forever, your great-great-great-great-grandchildren will be admiring all these things, too.

FAST is located just outside of Sparta on Highway 21 East near Highway Q. It's worth cruising past headquarters to view the graveyard of colossal roosters, cheeseburgers, hobos, and Holsteins. Or browse the awesome inventory at www.fastkorp.com.

Boys Clubs
Sparta

The Masons (the capitalized ones, though the lowercase ones came first, to do the groundwork) constructed the building that now houses the Monroe County Historical Society. In 1923 it was Sparta's first building devoted entirely to a social organization, and now that it's the county museum, the Local History Room recalls the Masons and other such groups with an exhibit called Sacred Objects of Secret Societies.

Now almost an endangered species, fraternal organizations like the Masons were flourishing a century ago, though their history goes back way further. It's as if guys needed an excuse to get out of the house to escape the womenfolk and then trumped up their importance with elaborate rituals, secret oaths, outlandish props and regalia, and a lot of Old Testament symbolism. Ornate robes were usually accessorized with swords, though the more down-to-earth Modern Woodmen of America preferred casual dress and axes. A local chapter of the Woodmen is featured here, including the stuffed goat used in initiation ceremonies (more about the frisky Woodmen on page 223). Once safely installed, Woodmen could look forward to a distinctive headstone in the shape of a tree stump, still seen in cemeteries across the nation.

Officials of the Knights of Pythias wore these costumes; the Woodmen and their stuffed goat dressed down.

The Masons and the Knights of Pythias are well represented here, too, but they were just downright mysterious. Times have changed, of course, and men seem to have less interest in or, since the 1970s, less choice about signing up for meetings that are all-male and mandatory.

The Monroe County Local History Room and Museum also has exhibits of medical equipment (such as a polio brace and Doc Williams's souvenir skull from medical school), old-time equipment from the firehouse, period dress, hair art, and much more. Upstairs is the Deke Slayton Memorial Space and Bicycle Museum, dedicated to Monroe County's own astronaut and to bicycles everywhere. See it all at 200 West Main Street. Visitor information at (608) 269-8680 and www.monroecountyhistory.org.

★ ★

The House of a Guy's Own

Spring Green

The House on the Rock is just a wee bit overdone. The carousel, for instance, has 20,000 lights, 182 chandeliers, 269 creatures (but not a single horse), and hundreds of mannequin-angels hovering and rotating overhead. There also are 250 dollhouses, miniature circuses with more than a million pieces, an organ console with fifteen keyboards, and tons of everything. At Christmas there are 6,000 Santas.

A tour of the extraordinary sixteen-building complex is like a movie made with a handheld camera. (Is this room moving?) The mix of music coming from all directions adds to the confusion, and together it has the quality of high school band practice.

By the time you stagger out three or four hours later, it's hard to name the strangest sight: The bushy eyebrows of a Fu Manchu drummer keeping time to "Danse Macabre" in the two-story Mikado exhibit? The carrying case for a woman's artificial leg, inlaid with a Derringer pistol, in Unique Weaponry? The soaring pipes, catwalks, and massive machinery in the cavelike Organ Room, to the tune of the "Anniversary Waltz"? The curious tableaux taking place within the dollhouses? The plaintive sight of an empty little rowboat in the jaw of the 200-foot sea creature in the six-story Heritage of the Sea? Ronald Reagan in the trumpet section of the life-size, eighty-piece, automated circus orchestra?

The tour opens in the Japanese-style stone house that Alex Jordan began building in the 1940s. Then in his thirties, Jordan was a job-hopping, ex-student, former cab driver from Madison. He favored low ceilings, dim lighting, carpeted surfaces instead of furniture, and fireplaces. To add to the seductive effect, a phantom chamber orchestra of bows saws away at Ravel's "Bolero." Several more such rooms lead to daylight and the Infinity Room, a 218-foot, glass-walled, cantilevered structure that soars out over the Wyoming Valley and offers a view of the valley floor, fifteen stories straight down.

The "expansion phase" represents Jordan's eccentric obsession to

★ ★

collect the largest, the biggest, and the most of whatever he came across—dolls, clocks, violins, mirrors, paperweights, weapons—and a place to put it all. Jordan never had enough of anything, and what he couldn't collect, he created. "It doesn't have to be good, it doesn't have to be bad, it just has to be," he often said. Much of what is here came from the on-site workshop.

The House on the Rock is one of Wisconsin's most mind-boggling and popular attractions. Open daily during the regular season, late April to early November. Also open in November and December for the scaled-down Christmas at House on the Rock. On Highway 23 between Spring Green and Dodgeville. Admission charge. Call (608) 935-3639 or visit www.thehouseontherock.com for details.

Circus musicians at House on the Rock wear Dodgeville High School band uniforms. WISCONSIN DEPARTMENT OF TOURISM

The Garden of Eden

You can't have missed the fact, thanks to J. Heileman Brewing, that Wisconsin is God's Country, but did you know it also was the site of the Garden of Eden? According to the Reverend D. O. Van Slyke of Galesville, his own Trempealeau County along the Mississippi matched the biblical description perfectly—four rivers, surrounding bluffs, hanging gardens, milk, honey, apples, and plenty of snakes, albeit rattle.

Van Slyke was a circuit-riding preacher whose ministry included spreading the word about the discovery of Eden at the confluence of Highways 53 and 54 and drawing the faithful back to the state of innocence. His 1886 pamphlet *Garden of Eden* made the case for the Wisconsin Eden, suggesting that Adam and Eve, having fallen from grace, moved to Minnesota (say, the Twin Cities—Sodom and Gomorrah?).

So That's What Happened to Anne Baxter

Spring Green

Now why would a tree in honor of Hollywood actress Anne Baxter (1924–1986) be growing in this rural cemetery, next to Unity Chapel? Because it's the Lloyd Jones family burial ground, and her mother, Catherine Wright Baxter, was architect Frank Lloyd Wright's first daughter, and Wright's mother was one of the "God-almighty Joneses," as the neighbors called them, for their high-mindedness and tendency to preside over the countryside ("Truth against the world" was the family motto).

Anne Baxter played such roles as Eve Harrington in *All About Eve* ("If nothing else, there's applause . . . like waves of love pouring over the

★ ★

footlights"), a princess of the Nile in *The Ten Commandments* ("Oh, Moses, you stubborn, splendid, adorable fool!"), and later on, for fun, Olga, Queen of the Cossacks, in several *Batman* episodes.

Frank Lloyd Wright's gravestone is here, but it marks an empty grave. He was buried here in 1959, but when his widow, Olgivanna, died in 1985, his body was removed and cremated so that his ashes could join hers at Taliesin West in Arizona, as her will specified.

The cemetery is 3 miles south of Spring Green, on Highway T, east of Highway 23.

First, Soak One Mountain
Trempealeau

Trempealeau Mountain rises out of the Mississippi River just north of town. Appropriately enough, the name means "mountain soaking in water." It's a solid-rock island, the tallest of three island-mountains along the Mississippi.

The mountain was an important landmark for early steamboat pilots. Today river travelers are more likely to think of this point in the river as Lock and Dam Number 6, one of five on the Wisconsin side.

Lockmaster is not a job for your basic Type A personality. It takes about two hours for a towboat to maneuver a barge through the locks—if all goes well—and five days for the 669-mile trip between St. Paul and St. Louis. Picture yourself sharing the highway with the fifty-eight trucks it would take to transport the same amount of cargo and give the barge captain a big smile.

You can watch the action from an observation tower between the Mississippi and the railroad tracks that run parallel to the river. Apparently this is a principal north–south route; freight trains roar through here about every thirty or forty minutes. A biking and hiking trail is also nearby. All in all, this would be a good place for scouts to work on their Transportation badge.

A plywood replica of the 9,000-year-old mastodon that was found near the village of Boaz in 1897 often appears in parades in Richland County on a Lions Club trailer. One side is painted to look like hair, the other side like bones. The skeleton of the big bruiser now stands in the Geology Museum at the University of Wisconsin–Madison. COURTESY BOAZ AREA LIONS CLUB

You're in Good Hands with Hüpeden

Valton

The community of Valton consists of just a handful of scattered buildings, and one of them is remarkable. On the outside, simple: white frame, 60 by 24 feet. On the inside, busy: every square inch is covered with a panoramic mural portraying the rituals and activities of the Modern Woodmen of America, a fraternal insurance society that flourished here around 1900.

It is the work of an itinerant landscape painter, Ernst Hupeden, who arrived in Valton in 1897 and was hired to paint the stage curtain for the Woodmen Meeting Hall. The Woodmen were so pleased and

impressed with the Mississippi River scene he produced that they asked him to continue. He agreed, in exchange for room and board and drink, according to one account of his life, which describes Hüpeden as "a colorful, tragic figure" whose past included emptying and painting whiskey bottles.

He went on to paint vivid scenes set in a pine forest that are both frightening depictions of injury and death (and life without life insurance?) and peaceful depictions of home life and fellowship among Woodmen. One scene shows a woman in mourning dress cashing in her insurance policy. Another reveals a curious initiation rite that involved strapping new members to a wooden goat on wheels and rolling them around the hall. (You can see one such goat at the Monroe County Local History Room and Museum; see page 218.)

Modern Woodmen evolved into today's Woodmen of the World, a financial institution. You may recall seeing its office tower in downtown Omaha in the opening scenes of *About Schmidt* as Warren R. Schmidt (Jack Nicholson) gloomily faces retirement from a top-notch job as a Woodmen actuary. No goats appear to be involved in the company's activities today.

Funding for the restoration of the Painted Forest was provided by the Kohler Foundation, which later turned it over to Edgewood College. It is open from 1 to 3 p.m. Saturday between Memorial Day and Labor Day. Call (608) 663-2307 to inquire about visiting at other times.

Cranberry Competition Bogs Down
Warrens

The annual Biggest Cranberry Contest is part of the three-day Warrens Cranberry Festival. Entries are judged by weight in grams. In case of a tie, the berries are measured for overall length, configuration, and originality of presentation to determine the winner.

Blue ribbons are awarded in ten different classes of cranberries. "Biggest Cranberry of Show" receives $25. (A recent "Biggest" weighed 5.08 grams. If that fails to impress you, weigh a few cranberries and read that line again.) Cranberries are displayed until the end of the festival on Sunday.

Wisconsin ranks first in U.S. cranberry production, and the War-rens gathering in late September is the largest cranberry festival in the world. It includes a parade, a fall produce market, several miles of antiques and crafts, marsh tours, and even cranberry royalty—little tiny red round people with regal bearing. Festival information is available at www.cranfest.com or (608) 378-4200.

A Living Flag
Witwen

The little community of Witwen consists of about twenty houses that face one another along two-lane Highway E. But neighbors come from miles around for Witwen's Fourth of July Parade. Lining up along the south edge of town, they point their vans toward the cornfields, pop their hatches, and set up lawn chairs behind the white line.

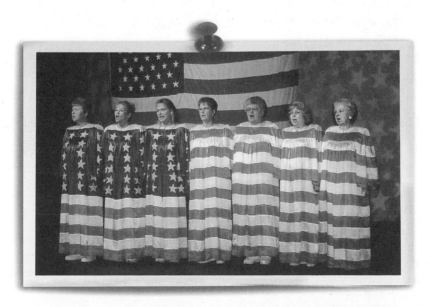

"She's a grand old flag . . ."
The Living Flag of Sauk County. COURTESY CAROL ANDERSON

★ ★

The Sauk Prairie High School band plays "This Is My Country," the Busy Badgers and the Happy Hustlers 4-H Clubs toss candy from their floats, and a great deal of farm machinery rolls by. But the high point of the parade is the Living Flag, a row of seven women marching shoulder to shoulder, dressed in satin robes that line up to form Old Glory. The tradition was started about fifty years ago.

The women who march today are members of the Sauk County Home and Community Education Association. They occasionally appear at other Wisconsin events, parades, or centennial celebrations. (But not if it looks like rain. Raindrops ruin satin.) They've been featured in the national media ever since Charles Kuralt discovered them On the Road in 1980, and they appear in Kuralt's video *Seasons of America.*

Witwen is 7 miles west of Sauk City. The parade begins at 10:30 a.m., followed by a church-sponsored chicken barbecue and family entertainment.

Who's There?

Wonewoc

The first Spiritualists arrived in Wonewoc in 1874, and for more than a century the land they purchased here has been the site of a summer camp. It's one of the thirteen camps of the National Spiritualist Association of Churches that give the general public a chance to experience the phenomena of Spiritualism, such as seeing dead people.

Spiritualists believe in communication with the so-called dead—"so-called" because, they say, a person's existence and identity continue after "the change called death." Highlights of a week at camp include the Spirit Message Circle (otherwise known as a séance), Past Life Regressions, and Table Tipping. There also are ice-cream socials, readings into the past and future (senior rates on Wednesday), and a gift shop. Campers live in rustic, historic cabins for only $15 to $30 a night. All of this takes place on thirty-seven wooded acres amid towering pines, shady oak trees, grazing deer, and hooting owls.

Judging by their bios and many years of experience, the mediums, healers, and readers on the staff are highly qualified. An ordained minister is clairvoyant, clairaudient, and clairsentient. Another minister has had extensive training in remote viewing. A Spiritual Channel discovered her gift after a car accident.

Spiritualists are positive, progressive, upbeat, nondogmatic, and accustomed to being made fun of. Citing the Golden Rule, their philosophy admires nature, supports freedom of religion, and opposes discrimination, war, and capital punishment. Add to that their belief that "there is no death, there are no dead," and it sounds as if they're definitely on the right track.

Wonewoc Spiritualist Camp is at 304 Hill Street, on a bluff above the town of Wonewoc. The season begins in June and ends toward the end of August. The camp's Web site, www.campwonewoc.com, gives more information, including a map, dates, and schedules.

appendix

★ ★

County, Community, and Area Tourism Contacts

Do you need information on lodging, attractions, or local events? Go
right to the source! Here we've listed some of Wisconsin's convention
bureaus, chambers of commerce, and county and area tourism offices.
These organizations are ready and waiting to help you plan your Wisconsin getaway.

Wisconsin Department of Tourism
(608) 266-2161 or (800) 432-8747
www.travelwisconsin.com

Adams County Chamber of Commerce
and Tourism
(608) 339-6997 or (888) 339-6997
www.adamscountywi.com

Antigo/Langlade County Chamber of
Commerce
(715) 623-4134 or (888) 526-4523
www.antigochamber.com

Appleton
(see Fox Cities)

Arbor Vitae
(see Minocqua-Arbor Vitae-Woodruff)

Ashland Area Chamber of Commerce
(715) 682-2500 or (800) 284-9484
www.visitashland.com

Baraboo Area Chamber of Commerce
(608) 356-8333 or (800) 227-2266
www.baraboo.com

Bayfield Chamber of Commerce
(715) 779-3335 or (800) 447-4094
www.bayfield.org

Bayfield County Tourism and Recreation
(715) 373-6125 or (800) 472-6338
www.travelbayfieldcounty.com

Beloit Convention and Visitors Bureau
(608) 365-4838 or (800) 423-5648
www.visitbeloit.com

Black River Falls Area Chamber of
Commerce
(715) 284-4658 or (800) 404-4008
www.blackrivercountry.net

Boscobel Chamber of Commerce
(608) 375-2672
www.boscobelwisconsin.com

Buffalo County Clerk's Office
(608) 685-6209
www.buffalocounty.com

Burnett County Dept. of Tourism
and Information
(715) 349-5999 or (800) 788-3164
www.burnettcounty.com

Cable Area Chamber of Commerce
(715) 798-3833 or (800) 533-7454
www.cable4fun.com

Calumet County) Travel Calumet
(920) 849-1493 ext. 200
www.travelcalumet.com

Chippewa Falls Area Visitors Center
(715) 723-0331 or (888) 723-0024
www.chippewachamber.org

Chippewa Valley Convention and Visitors
Bureau
(715) 831-2345 or (888) 523-3866
www.chippewavalley.net

Columbia Co Tourism and Economic
Development
(608) 742-6161 or (800) 842-2524
http://fun.co.columbia.wi.us

Columbus Area Chamber of Commerce
(920) 623-3699
www.cityofcolumbuswi.com

Cornell or City of
(715) 239-3710
www.cityofcornell.com

Delavan-Delavan Lake Area Chamber of
Commerce
(262) 728-5095 or (800) 624-0052
www.delavanwi.org

Dodge County Tourism Association
(920) 386-3701 or (800) 414-0101
www.dodgecounty.com

Dodgeville Area Chamber of Commerce
(608) 935-9200 or (877) 863-6343
www.dodgeville.com

Door County Chamber of Commerce
(920) 743-4456 or (800) 527-3529
www.doorcounty.com

Douglas County
(see Superior-Douglas County)

Eau Claire
(see Chippewa Valley)

Fennimore Chamber and Economic Devel
opment Office
(608) 822-3599 or (800) 822-1131
www.fennimore.com

Florence County Tourism
(715) 528-5377 or (888) 889-0049
www.florencewisconsin.com

Fond du Lac Area Convention and Visitors
Bureau
(920) 923-3010 or (800) 937-9123
www.fdl.com

Fort Atkinson Area Chamber of Commerce
(920) 563-3210 or (888) 733-3678
www.fortchamber.com

Fox Cities Convention and Visitors Bureau
(920) 734-3358 or (800) 236-6673
www.foxcities.org

Galesville
(see Trempealeau County)

Germantown Area Chamber of Commerce
(262) 255-1812
www.germantownchamber.org

Glidden Area Chamber of Commerce
(715) 264-4304

Grant County UWEX Office
(608) 723-2125 or (866) 472-6894
www.grantcounty.org/visitor

Grantsburg Chamber of Commerce
(715) 463-2405
www.grantsburgwi.com

Green Bay Convention and Visitor Bureau,
Greater
(920) 494-9507 or (888) 867-3342
www.packercountry.com

Green County Tourism
(608) 328-1838 or (888) 222-9111
www.greencounty.org

Hayward Lakes Visitors and Convention
Bureau
(715) 634-4801 or (800) 724-2992
www.haywardlakes.com

Hudson Area Chamber of Commerce and
Tourism Bureau
(715) 386-8411 or (800) 657-6775
www.hudsonwi.org

Iron River Area Chamber of Commerce
(715) 372-8558 or (800) 345-0716
www.iracc.com

Jackson County
(see Black River Area)

Jefferson County Area Tourism Council
(920) 563-3210
www.jctourism.com

Juneau County Visitors Bureau/Economic
Development
(608) 847-1904
www.juneaucounty.com/tourism.asp

Kaukauna
(see Fox Cities)

Kenosha Area Convention and Visitors
Bureau
(262) 654-7307 or (800) 654-7309
www.kenoshacvb.com

Kewaunee Chamber of Commerce
(920) 388-4822 or (800) 666-8214
www.kewaunee.org

Kewaunee County Promotions and Recreation Department
(920) 388-0444

Kohler Visitor Information Center
(920) 458-3450
www.destinationkohler.com

La Crosse Area Convention and Visitors
Bureau
(608) 782-2366 or (800) 658-9424
www.explorelacrosse.com

Lac du Flambeau Chamber of Commerce
(715) 588-3346 or (877) 588-3346
www.lacduflambeauchamber.com

Lake Geneva Area Convention and Visitors
Bureau
(262) 248-4416 or (800) 345-1020
www.lakegenevawi.com

Lake Mills Area Chamber of Commerce
(920) 648-3585
www.lakemills.org

Lake Tomahawk Information Bureau
(715) 277-2602

Langlade County
(see Antigo Area)

Lincoln County Forestry, Land and Parks
(715) 536-0327
www.co.lincoln.wi.us

Madeline Island Chamber of Commerce
(715) 747-2801 or (888) 475-3386
www.madelineisland.com

Madison Convention and Visitors Bureau,
Greater
(608) 255-2537 or (800) 373-6376
www.visitmadison.com

Manitowish Waters Chamber of
Commerce
(715) 543-8488 or (888) 626-9877
www.manitowishwaters.org

Manitowoc Area Visitor and Convention
Bureau
(920) 683-4388 or (800) 627-4896
www.manitowoc.info

appendix

Manitowoc-Two Rivers Area Chamber of
Commerce
(920) 684-5575 or (800) 262-7892
www.manitowocchamber.com

Marinette/Menominee Area Chamber of
Commerce
(715) 735-6681 or (800) 236-6681
www.marinettechamber.com

Marquette County Clerk's Office
(608) 297-9136

Marshfield Convention and Visitors Bureau
(715) 384-3454 or (800) 422-4541
www.visitmarshfieldwi.com

Menasha
(see Fox Cities)

Menominee Tribal Public Relations
(715) 799-5217

Milton Area Chamber of Commerce
(608) 868-6222
www.maccit.com

Milwaukee, VISIT
(414) 273-7222 or (800) 554-1448
www.milwaukee.org

Minocqua-Arbor Vitae-Woodruff Area
Chamber of Commerce
(715) 356-5266 or (800) 446-6784
www.minocqua.org

Monroe Chamber of Commerce and
Industry
(608) 325-7648
wicip.uwplatt.edu/green/ci/monroe

Montello Area Chamber of Commerce
(608) 297-7420 or (800) 684-7199
www.montellowi.com

Mount Horeb Area Chamber of
Commerce
(608) 437-5914 or (888) 765-5929
www.trollway.com

Neenah
(see Fox Cities)

Neillsville Area Chamber of Commerce
(715) 743-6444 or (888) 252-7594
www.neillsville.org

New Glarus Chamber of Commerce and
Tourist Information
(608) 527-2095 or (800) 527-6838
www.swisstown.com

Oconomowoc Convention and Visitors
Bureau
(262) 569-3236 or (800) 524-3744
www.oconomowocusa.com

Oconto County Tourism
(920) 834-6969 or (888) 626-6862
www.ocontocounty.org

Osceola Area Chamber of Commerce
(715) 755-3300 or (800) 947-0581
www.osceolachamber.org

Oshkosh Convention and Visitors Bureau
(920) 303-9200 or (877) 303-9200
www.oshkoshcvb.org

Ozaukee County Tourism Council
(262) 284-9288 or (800) 403-9898
www.ozaukeetourism.com

Pepin County Visitor Information
(715) 672-5709 or (888) 672-5709
www.pepinwisconsin.com

Phillips Area Chamber of Commerce
(715) 339-4100 or (888) 408-4800
www.phillipswisconsin.net

Pierce County Partners in Tourism, Inc.
(715) 273-5864 or (800) 474-3723
www.travelpiercecounty.com

Platteville Area Chamber of Commerce
(608) 348-8888
www.platteville.com

Polk County Information Center
(715) 483-1410 or (800) 222-7655
www.polkcountytourism.com

Prairie du Chien Area Chamber of
Commerce
(608) 326-8555 or (800) 732-1673
www.prairieduchien.org

Price County Tourism Dept.
(715) 339-4505 or (800) 269-4505
www.pricecountywi.net

Princeton Area Chamber of Commerce
(920) 295-3877
www.princetonwi.com

Racine County Convention and Visitors
Bureau
(262) 884-6400 or (800) 272-2463
www.racine.org

Richland Center Area Chamber/Main
Street
(608) 647-6205
www.richlandchamber.com

Ripon Area Chamber of Commerce
(920) 748-6764
www.ripon-wi.com

Rock County Tourism Council
(608) 757-5587 or (866) 376-8767
www.rockcounty.org

Rusk County Visitors Center and Rail
Displays
(715) 532-2642 or (800) 535-7875
www.ruskcounty.org

Sauk Prairie Area Chamber of Commerce
(608) 643-4168 or (800) 683-2453
www.saukprairie.com

Sayner-Star Lake Chamber of Commerce
(715) 542-3789 or (888) 722-3789
www.sayner-starlake.org

Sheboygan County Chamber of
Commerce
(800) 457-9497
www.sheboygan.org

Shell Lake Chamber of Commerce
(715) 468-4340
www.shelllakeonline.com

Shullsburg Community Development
Corporation
(608) 965-4579
www.shullsburgwisconsin.org

Sister Bay Advancement Association
(920) 854-2812
www.sisterbaytourism.com

Sparta Area Chamber of Commerce
(608) 269-4123 or (800) 354-2453
www.bikesparta.com

Spooner Area Chamber of Commerce
(715) 635-2168 or (800) 367-3306
http://chamber.spooneronline.com

Spring Green Chamber of Commerce
(608) 588-2054 or (800) 588-2042
www.springgreen.com

Sun Prairie Chamber of Commerce
(608) 837-4547 or (800) 400-6162
www.sunprairiechamber.com

appendix

Superior-Douglas County Convention and Visitors Bureau
(715) 392-2773 or (800) 942-5313
www.superiorchamber.org

Taylor County Tourism
(715) 748-4729 or (888) 682-9567
www.medfordwis.com

Trempealeau Chamber of Commerce
(608) 534-6780
www.trempealeau.net

Trempealeau County Tourism Council
(608) 534-6615 or (800) 927-5339
www.trempealeaucountytourism.com

Two Rivers
(see Manitowoc Area VCB)

Uplands of Southwest Wisconsin
(608) 437-6580 or (800) 279-9472
www.uplands.ws

Vernon County Tourism Council
(608) 637-2575
www.visitvernoncounty.com

Vilas County Advertising and Publicity Dept.
(715) 479-3649 or (800) 236-3649
www.vilas.org

Walworth County Visitor's Bureau
(262) 723-3980 or (800) 395-8687
www.visitwalworthcounty.com

Warrens Area Business Association
(608) 378-4200
www.cranfest.com

Washburn County/Spooner Area Tourism
(715) 635-9696 or (800) 367-3306
www.washburncounty.org

Washington County Convention and Visitors Bureau
(262) 677-5069 or (888) 974-8687
www.visitwashingtoncounty.com

Washington Island Chamber of Commerce
(920) 847-2179
www.washingtonislandchamber.com

Watertown Area Chamber of Commerce
(920) 261-6320
www.watertownchamber.com

Waukesha and Pewaukee CVB
(262) 542-0330 or (800) 366-8474
www.visitwaukesha.org

Wausau-Central Wisconsin Convention and Visitors Bureau
(715) 355-8788 or (888) 948-4748
www.visitwausau.com

Wisconsin Dells Visitor and Convention Bureau
(608) 254-4636 or (800) 223-3557
www.wisdells.com

Wisconsin Indian Head Country Tourism
(715) 924-2970 or (800) 826-6966
www.wisconsinindianhead.org

Wisconsin Rapids Area Convention and Visitors Bureau
(715) 422-4650 or (800) 554-4484
www.visitwisrapids.com

Woodruff
(see Minocqua-Arbor Vilae-Woodruff)

index

index

index

index

index

index

index

index

index

index

about the authors

Michael Feldman has been doing radio for the better or worse part of twenty-plus years, most of it spent producing and hosting *Michael Feldman's Whad'Ya Know?* on Public Radio International. He lives in Madison, Wisconsin, with one wife, Sandy; two daughters, Ellie and Nora; and two dogs, Sugar and Tina.

Diana Cook researches the burning issues and inside dope for the cities of *Michael Feldman's Whad'Ya Know?*'s road shows and does freelance editorial work in Madison. She is the author of *Wisconsin Capitol: Fascinating Facts* and several features in *The Wisconsin Almanac,* and she recently revised and updated *Wisconsin Trivia.* She lives in Madison, and her children are Andrew and Julia.